Destined to Live

Destined to Live

Morella Reece

*Edited by Dr Antonia MacDonald-Smythe
and Mrs Deborah Lambert*

Copyright © 2007 by Morella Reece.

| ISBN: | Hardcover | 978-1-4257-7444-8 |
| | Softcover | 978-1-4257-7438-7 |

This book was printed in the United States of America.

To order additional copies of this book, contact:
Xlibris Corporation
1-888-795-4274
www.Xlibris.com
Orders@Xlibris.com
38414

Contents

@@@

DEDICATION

Destined To Live is dedicated to my husband Merlin Da Costa Reece; my children Charlene Morella Reece, Darwin Da Costa Reece; my extended family Debora Reece Augustin, Tony Cyril Reece, Jason Levi Leon; my mother Sarah Ishmael; my sister Pamela Epiphane; my cousins Cecile Smith, Christina Duncan, Marcella and Shirley; my uncle Bertie Amedee—who stuck with me through 'thick and thin'. I had almost given up as contrary circumstances seemed to negate what God has said.

@@@

A NOTE FROM THE AUTHOR

The main reason for writing this book is to help people who may be afflicted with depression or cancer, or any other sickness or disease, and have either given up, or are contemplating on 'throwing in the towel'. I say to you **DO NOT GIVE UP**. Even if the doctor has looked at you and said that there is nothing more that he can do for you, take courage. Worse still, the doctor might have sent you home to die, I say again **DO NOT GIVE UP**.

Most doctors are very good, and I thank God for them, but they do not have the last word—God has. You may feel distant from the Omnipotent One, and the more you pray and cry out to Him, the more it may appear that He becomes distant. Keep on praying, keep on crying. God's timing is not like man's. We are living in an instant world which teaches us not to wait. Instant coffee, instant potatoes, microwave. Give it to me, and do that quick. I say, wait on the Lord. Pray without ceasing. Sometimes while praying you may run short of words. Groan, the Holy Spirit will take the groaning and interpret it to God. When all else fails, read the instructions—the word of God. It will direct your steps. Hope in God the Father, for He never fails. Wait on Him and be patient. Remember, **IT IS NOT OVER, UNTIL GOD SAYS THAT IT IS OVER.**

IN GRATITUDE

This book would not be complete if I do not thank my biological family, church family, work mates, friends, neighbors, relatives, doctors, and everyone who helped in one way or other while I was sick and on my way to recovery. You will not go unrewarded for your thoughtfulness, your patience, your kindness and your love. Thank you for not giving up on me.

Merlin, Charlene and Darwin Reece
Dr Wendy & Sylvester Reece
Eleanor Collymore
Trevor Francis
Sherwin Griffith
Rebecca Alexander
Anya Alexander
Dr Antonia Smythe
Dr Charles Greenidge
Josephine Romain
Yolande Trim
Annette Lucien
Ursuline (Sandra) Hallpike & Titin
Christina Duncan
Unifa Joseph
Lydia Joseph
Susan John
Angela and Kenneth Henry
Gregory and Gilma Lionel

I could not have succeeded without your help. My desire is that while people read this book and be blessed, that Our Heavenly Father will also bless you for your invaluable assistance. I love and appreciate you all.

I hope I have helped someone by writing this book. God Bless!!!
In the Master's service,

Morella Reece

CHAPTER ONE

HOW IT ALL BEGAN

My Conception

As I reminisce, I recognize that Satan has been hurling his darts at me from conception. I am one of my father's illegitimates. When I had enough sense to understand who I really was, I bombarded my mother with numerous questions. One of them was, why wasn't she married to my father. I was told that I was the third of four children. The first, a boy named Andrew died a few days after birth. My sister Pamela was born second, I appeared on the scene two years later and my brother, Malcolm was born seven years after me.

My mother said that she always intended to marry, and never enjoyed living a life in fornication. My father, who is now deceased, promised to marry her, but could not do so. During her pregnancy with me, one of her cherished friends greeted her with some shocking news. My father was indeed married, and his wife and children had arrived in the state from Barbados. At first my mother said that she was speechless. With one child just over one year old, one in her womb, and not having a husband, the news devastated her. The first piece of advice from that trusted friend was, "Rhona, don't make another child for that man. You already have one, and the man is not yours, kill that child." Yes that was me, kill me, kill Morella. That friend later brought her a concoction for the abortion.

The bottle for the abortion was laid on a shelf in the bedroom, and the big decision had to be made. About three days after the mixture was delivered, and amidst several calls from her friend enquiring whether she had drank the contents of the bottle, my mother told me that she was lying on the bed in a very pensive mood. She was wondering whether she should drink the mixture or not. She was also in a confused state of mind. Something was telling her to drink the mixture, while something else was telling her not to drink it. She finally made up her mind. **SHE DECIDED NOT TO DRINK IT.** My life was spared, and I must have breathed a sigh of relief in the womb. I must have also attempted to shout a few hallelujahs with my unformed mouth. My temporary home must have moved a little bit, as I expressed the joy of living. ***I will live, praise the Lord, I will live, thank you mummy, thank you. Devil you lose, big time.***

The pregnancy went through to full term, without joy and excitement. Fancy layette was not prepared for me like my sister, but I got a few bits and pieces that were not stylish at all, without embroidery. I also got a few 'hand me downs' from my sister's. June 4th 1955 finally came and I was born. A splitting image of my mom. I was a bit fair, with red hair, a flat nose and looking good. Francisca Morella Reece was born. I am not very happy for the manner in which I was conceived, but I am extremely happy to be born. I had no choice in my conception, and I am not an accident. ***I am fearfully and wonderfully made*** (Ps. 139:14) and so I cannot be blamed.

My Childhood Days

I was taken to Wilton's Yard (on the Chaussee) which is now called The Graveyard. I grew up there and attended Miss Lucy's preschool. At Miss Lucy, there was not much glamour. At that time it was situated where Burger Plus is now situated. I recall the days when school was about to close, Miss Lucy would invite some "magic men" to entertain us. They performed acts like eating fire, walking on hot coals, putting small pieces of paper in their mouths, and pulling out yards and yards of paper.

Miss Lucy occupied a small area which was elevated from the main floor. From that position she could have supervised the entire school. She also loved to punish us with a belt named Johnny which I felt a few times. In those days, there was hardly any other form of punishment exercised apart from the strap (belt).

At that time, I played a great deal at home, at school and with the neighbours. The place where I lived made it easy for me to play. Being close to Chaussee Road where the action was, made it very easy for me to hear and see things. It was a main route for carnival bands, funerals, all types of marches and demonstrations. We invited friends to our house and frequently visited relatives in the country. My mom took us places as well to visit her friends, where we met children to play with. She took us on Columbus Square, now Derek Walcott's Square, during the New Year activities, until we could have gone by ourselves. We were also taken there on some nights, just to run around and buy ice cream.

My Major Accident

While attending Miss Lucy's school, I was involved in a major accident. If I was not destined to live, I would have died instantly. We had a housekeeper whom my mother had sent to the shop at lunch time to buy her some onions. I was around that afternoon, and asked whether I could accompany her to the shop. She took me along and was holding my hand. After a short while, she suggested that we run a race to see who would reach the shop first. She dashed across the street before me and the car missed her. I collided with a bicycle which flew me onto the upcoming vehicle. The car hit me on the head, and I found myself beneath it. The car passed on my hair, not my head (a plait stayed on the road). Thank God! My brains could have stayed on the road, but the devil lost another time.

I was taken to Victoria Hospital where I stayed unconscious for seven days. When I woke up, I recall feeling my skin burning, and it was very bumpy. This was because bed bugs had bitten me all over my body. I also recall being given a glass of warm milk. The doctor who handled my case said to my mom that as a result of the blow to my head, I would be somewhat retarded. I would not be able to cope at school, and I would suffer from severe headaches. I thank God that he had a better plan for me. God turned all this around and gave me a miracle. The doctor was not wrong. The devil meant to kill or cripple me, but all things worked together for my good. (Rom.8:28). Thank God that I am not a vegetable and that I am not retarded today. God had alternative plans.

CHAPTER TWO

SCHOOL DAYS & ADOLESCENT YEARS

Anglican Infant

Infant school was great except for the feelings in my body that I experienced when I wrote on the slate with the pencil. It made "my blood crawl". I thank God for the day that I graduated to pen and paper. Mrs. Collymore and Miss Boxill were the head teachers at that school. My most vivid memory of them is when they used to stand at the gate awaiting late comers. They would beat them from the very gate before they asked for an excuse. They were disciplinarians who desired all their students to excel.

Anglican Primary

Primary school days with Mr. Keith Weekes were much more exciting. Mr. Weekes was fun to be with. When it was singing time on a Friday, his two favorite songs which had also become the school's favorite would be sung first. They were: *In the Gloaming Oh My Darling* and *Juanita*. We would all listen to Mr. Weekes as he sang, smiled and swayed. Today, I still sing those songs and feel the same chills that I felt when I was a little girl. Mr. Weekes used a method which worked for the school. He knew how to compliment his students. Whenever we did well, he praised us, and of course when we did the wrong things, he punished us.

Ursuline (Sandra) Mitchell and I would sing hymns at school concerts, and have the school encourage us to sing again. Imagine singing a hymn like: *Just as I am Without One Plea* at a concert in those days. Sandra sang alto and I soprano. If someone does that at a concert today, he or she would either be booed, or chased out, as the audience would shout, "Outside, outside."

Make sure that you make it to heaven Mr. Weekes. I understand that the angels will fold their wings when the blood-washed sing. I further understand that those who now crow and croak will have melodious voices in heaven.

When children were eleven and twelve in my days, it was the children of the elite who were chosen to sit the Common Entrance exam. Children were hand-picked, and excuses were given for those who were not chosen. The excuses given were that they were either too old, or they were not bright enough. I ended up at the SDA Academy after doing credibly in my exams.

While at the Anglican Primary School, I sat in a teacher's class in Standard Three (now Grade Five). When it was time to say our tables, it was also time for licks (lashes with the belt). We sang the two times tables to the twelve times. I knew them so I did not get lashes.

I vividly remember one particular day at school, that was the day after which I was absent due to illness. In my absence, long division was taught to the class. The day I came to school, there were two examples of Long division on the black-board. When I saw the expression on the teacher's face and the belt in her hand, I knew what that meant. Since I did not know what to do, I copied from David, a new student from Barbados. I felt that I had achieved something, since I completed the exercise. I felt relaxed as I sat on the bench in the front row with six other students.

The teacher began correcting the sums as she passed around. She corrected the sums of three of the girls in the front row first; they got them correct. She then came to David. He too had it correct, but he had worked it a different way—the Bajan way. When she uttered that it was correct but different, I became frightened since I had copied on David. The teacher then checked my book, and before I could explain that I was absent, she asked, "So you are a Bajan too?" and it was 'Licks can't done'. My teacher punished me in order to teach me that I should not copy. To my surprise, the two other girls after me had copied from me, too, so there were four Bajans in the class that day!

Secondary School Days

The Seventh Day Adventist Academy (SDAA) under the command of Mr. Hill and Mr. Mason with the assistance of stars like Walston Charles, Cyrus Reynolds, Miss Kelsick, Lena and Ruth Williams, Mrs. Bovel, the Mathurins, the Joneses, Mr. Menard, Mr. Robert Innocent and others were the best. Those teachers mothered and fathered us. They were our friends, worship leaders and confidantes. They taught us well. I fondly remember the songs that we sang during worship sessions: *Lord in the Morning, This is my Father's World, and I Sing the Mighty Power of God.* Those songs were ethereal, and while we sung them, God endowed us with His presence. I believe that was the reason why our school was so unique.

God wanted me at the SDA Academy. While there, some important values were instilled into me that have helped to mould me into the person that I am today. I was transformed into a much better person. The teachers were great and I esteem them highly to this day. Most of them are still stalwarts in our society.

One day, the principal, Mr. Mason, called me into his office because my skirt was two inches above the knee instead of the recommended two inches below the knee. He said to me, "Morella, a blind man in a dark room, with dark shades on, and looking through tinted glass windows could notice that your skirt is too short, so do something about it." I gasped for breath, I did not recognize that the skirt seemed so short to him. That afternoon I had an assignment to take down the hem of all my uniforms. Wow, when I see children going to school with short skirts I remember Mr. Mason, "Sa Gam" (no shape), his nickname, and say to myself that they need a lecture from him.

At the school, we had no laboratory. We examined cockroaches on our desks, and slit frogs the same place. If we had a proper laboratory, many more of us would have written Biology. I sat it one year with Cambridge after I left school and got a "C". I'm one of those who needed a modern lab to obtain a better grade.

My Conversion

Ursuline (Sandra) Mitchell, my dear and precious friend for many years invited me to Sunday School when I was about eleven years old. From the first day, I got hooked. It was in a very small church, but the warmth and friendliness that I felt was indescribable. I liked the people very much. Although one would consider the structure of the church as a "two by four", I was prepared from the first day to leave my big church and be with those people. I fell in love with the singing. From then on I would go to my big church on a Sunday, and after the mass was over, I would run to the small church so that I would not miss much of the chorus session in Sunday School.

I surrendered my life to the Lord at an early age, fourteen, and was very much interested in the things of God. I was also baptized in water at that age. At one point, my mother, not knowing any better, felt that I was too interested in that small church, and started to apply pressure on me. She told me one day that I was not going back to that church, and when I went to bed in the night, I cried until it appeared that I had no more tears. When she saw how determined I was, and the drastic change in my behavior, she had no choice but to let me serve my God. I lived to see that she too came into the fold.

How We Lived

While we were very young my mother managed a small bakery which was located in proximity to our house. It was called a brick oven in those days, and there were a few workers employed. I can recall waking up on mornings to the aroma of fresh local bread and cakes. As a child, I enjoyed serving the customers during which time I made many friends. My mother also worked hard as a seamstress. My father visited us on weekends with his meager allowance. At that time, I thought he was stingy when it came to the allowance, but now that I am grown, I realize that he was depriving his legitimates of this money when he gave it to us.

After all, we were the 'bastards'. I thank God that he gave it anyway. My father also gave us change to purchase our junk, and I really loved him for that. He would also give money to any child that was home when he visited. My mother struggled to give us a decent life. She is a fighter to this day. She could have had many worldly possessions, but she sacrificed a lot for our sakes, and today we honor her. I vowed to take care of her when she can no longer take care of herself, and as long as I am alive and able, no old age home will have her. She has informed us that she will live for two hundred years, so help us God. If the Lord tarries, I will have to make arrangements for the great, and great, great grand children to continue to take care of her after I am gone. My mother fought among all the persecutions from her enemies. We were called second hand and 'ration' children, but the good Lord was with us.

While my mom and the bakers were working hard at preparing bread for the next day, we, the children, were having some good fun at home. One of our favorite games was 'wosh' (stone). We would wet bread (the round rolls) wrap it in a cloth until it got hard like rock. At nights, we threw the hard bread at each other saying, 'wosh' as we blocked the effects of the knocks with pillows. Once in a while, our heads took some real hard knocks. A second game was 'Ride the bicycle in the corner'. For this game, two persons would lie on their backs in opposite directions with the flat part of their feet together. Their legs would move from side to side as they do the motions of riding a bicycle and sang, "Ride, ride, ride your bicycle in the corner." The third and favorite game was "Rocka my baby". That game required three persons. Two persons would hold the ends of a sheet, whilst the third would lie in the middle. The two persons would stand on a bed and swing the sheet as they sang, 'Rocka by baby.' After swinging for a few minutes the person would be thrown down onto a waiting mattress on the floor. One night, I passed through the sheet. All of us tried to mend it with needle and thread before my mother came in for the night. We hid it of course, and did not play that game for a long time.

During our young days, my mom wanted to find out whether we were little thieves. She tested us by placing a ten-cent piece on a ledge near our bed. The money stayed there for about two weeks, nobody took it. The ten-cent piece was placed on the dining room table for a few days, and again nobody touched it. It reappeared on the ledge near our bed and my sister felt that that money had no owner, so she took it. She suffered for it later.

My Family

Sarah, My Precious Mom

The best woman on planet earth with whom God chose that I should live, my mother. She decided not to abort me when the devil planned to kill me. I have emulated her a great deal. She is one of a kind, and she is indeed unique. One will look far and wide, and will not come up with such a strong woman; that strength is physical, emotional and spiritual. We almost lost her in December 1983. She was in a diabetic coma in the United States for a few days. I can't remember praying more earnestly than I prayed at that time. Thank God He spared her life.

Before my mother became a Christian, my sister-in-law, Mrs. Eleanor Collymore looked at her one day and said to her, "Rhona you are too good to go to hell." I think that was her turning point in deciding to live for the Lord, and not the Devil. The message was short, one more word than Jonah's message when he went to preach in Ninevah (Jonah 3:4), but that was all Rhona needed to be converted. Thank God! Thank Eleanor!

My mom said she looked at me one day whilst I was leading the church in a song session and she said, "My God, look at what I would have killed." She said that she started to cry, and could have hardly contain herself. I thank God so much that she chose to let me live.

My Sister, Pamela

Growing up with my sister was a lot of fun. I was the one who was always in charge. I made most of the decisions, and people used to be confused as to who the older one was. We are very close to this day. She now resides in the United States, and I visit her quite often. When we meet, we always talk about the good old days, and usually 'laugh our hearts out'. My sister is happily married with four children.

My Brother, Malcolm

When my brother, Malcolm, was born, he was something for the eyes to behold and feast on. He was handsome, smooth-skinned, and a joy to his sisters. Mr. Horace who is Malcolm's father, lived with us. He was a good man who loved and respected us. He treated us as though we were his biological children. We grew up without our own father living in the same house as us, but my mother did a good job.

After my step father started to misbehave, my mother asked him to leave. We cried a lot when he left, since he had spoilt us, and he was so much fun to be with. We then had to settle down to a life of single parenting. Given the circumstances, my mother could not have done a better job. She commanded our respect, and to this day, we honor her. We were always looked up to in our community. We were not the richest, although some people thought that we were. We held our heads up high when we walked. We had a lot of fun growing up, and my mother played with us sometimes. However, I missed a father figure in our home as a child.

When I saw dads walking along the sidewalk with their children, especially little girls, my heart used to hurt. I vowed at that tender age that when I have children that I would ensure that they had a father who would stay. One who would also play with them. God gave me my heart's desire. My children are now adults, their father has always been there, and we have not stopped the playing either. When they were children, I would sometimes hear them beckoning their father to stop teasing them. They would say things like, "daddy behave", or "daddy what scene are you on?" or "cool out." While they were growing up, we played numerous games including floor games, board games and many games in our yard. The homes in which we lived were open to many, and our yard was a playground for many children in the community. Our children still talk about the quality time that we spent together. We enjoyed every moment.

My Cousin, Florence

Florence lived with us for a few years while we lived on the Chaussee. She is a precious gem. When she came home from the country she could have done everything at her young age—cooking, washing and ironing. Unlike her, we could have only clean the house and make up a bed.

We grew up as sisters, wore the same clothes, slept in the same bed and protected each other. I vividly remember the day a girl hit me during break time at school and I sent for my cousin, Florence. She did not hesitate to come. When she arrived on the scene, she just asked "which one?" and when the girl was identified, she immediately positioned her pencil. She pricked the girl in the forehead, breaking the point of the pencil. Foy, (as she is affectionately called) did not hesitate to use her weapon. That caused a lot of trouble, and someone called the headmistress when she saw the girl bleeding. Well, the case was then between Florence, the girl, her parents and the headmistress.

After the case was over, the girl was taken to the hospital. Florence was severely beaten, and put to stand on the bench for the balance of the day. I went along playing with my friends without any sympathy. After all, I was the reason why she had found herself in that predicament. After lunch, Florence had to return to her punish spot. Every time I passed near her with my friends, she would 'cut her eyes' at me. The school day was finally ended, and she was relieved from her elevated position.

Florence was afraid of worms, and my sister and I made sure that we saved a few whenever we shelled pigeon peas. We would run after Florence all through the neighborhood, even after the worms had fallen off the pod. Florence often sided with my sister against me, and running after her with worms was one of the ways I used to get even with her. She is now married, has her own unique family, and continues to inspire us. She is a great source of spiritual strength.

CHAPTER THREE

ADULT LIFE

Joining the Workforce

Though school days were great, every student looked forward in eagerness and apprehension towards working days. We could hardly wait to leave the school bench. Throwing stones at Gordon's mangoes had finally come to an end for us, and it was job-hunting time after five years of secondary school education. I walked for six months, finished three pairs of shoes until I found myself in the Prime Minister's office. I poured my frustrations of job hunting to him, and to my surprise he was sympathetic. I thought that men of such caliber did not care much about lowly citizens.

He listened, and to my surprise started to make telephone calls in my presence. "My God", I said to myself, "what a man!" I fell in love with him from that day. I was tired of hearing the usual choruses like "your name is on file" or "no vacancies." The Prime Minister sent me to a few places, and after about the fourth week he asked me, "Miss Philgence, where do you really want to work?' I replied, "At The Government's Treasury." He called the Accountant General who asked to send me to him. The Prime Minister called me three (3) days later and asked me to report to work on the following Monday. I will never forget this gesture as long as I live. I sent two of my friends to him later, told them what to say, and how to say it, and to this day, both of them are in the Government Service. I have always kept in touch with Sir John, and I will be forever grateful. He is one of the most important people in my life today, and I love and respect him.

Treasury Days

At the Treasury, I worked as a Junior Clerk for three years before I was promoted to Senior Clerk. I was responsible for the salaries of all teachers in the state. I enjoyed working there. The payroll clerks were very nice people. Miss Anne Marie Alexander who was the Accountant General of the Treasury then was a real beautiful person, too. She was always there for us. She chatted with us, and fed us during overtime nights and on

Saturdays. Miss Alexander died many years ago, and I miss her greatly. It is said that good people do not remain on planet earth for too long, and it is the miserable ones who stay on. This is not biblically correct. The good book encourages us to honor our father and mother that our days may be long (Deut.5:16).

National Insurance Scheme (NIS) Days, Now (NIC) National Insurance Corporation

After seven and a half years of hard labor at the Government Treasury, I stayed home for nine months before I started work at the National Insurance Scheme. Every woman who has had a child knows how it feels when the time comes to return to work, leaving your baby for someone else to care for. I wanted to spend some time with Charlene, so I took leave for a few months. However, there came a time when the saying, "a woman's place is in the home" was not working for me, and I applied for a job at the National Insurance Scheme. After a few hurdles were removed, I was hired. I was promoted in less than six (6) months, and God has been there for me all the time. I am presently serving as an Investigating Officer. I look forward to the day when I will not have to report to anyone, but have and run my own business.

How I Met My Husband

After I settled at the Treasury, I began to seriously consider my future with my then boyfriend of two years, Merlin Da Costa Reece. He found me in church. We loved each other dearly. That flat nose, not so pretty girl had attracted a flat nose good-looking man. (We were attracted by the noses). Merlin was very kind and sensitive. He was, and still is a gentleman who can win the heart of any woman. God hand-picked us for each other. When I agreed to marry Merlin, this was one of the best and biggest decisions I made in my life.

I am eternally grateful to God for helping me in making this choice. Some guys were interested in me around the same time that Merlin made his move. I brushed them off since Merlin overshadowed them all. When he told me that I was beautiful, I chuckled. After he left, I looked in a mirror and had a good laugh. However, Merlin meant every word that he said. It is said that beauty is in the eyes of the beholder, and after thirty years of marriage, he still woos me with these words. He sometimes says, "Darling you are very precious and beautiful, and I love you." I have never gotten tired of hearing it. I now believe that I am beautiful, and forget what others think. Case closed!!! After four (4) years of courtship, I heard our wedding bells ringing. Myrl and Moy (our flattered names) were joined together in holy matrimony at Bocage by our now deceased Bishop H.T. Gentles of Barbados. Bishop Carlisle Collymore was my father giver, and Mr. Ulric Reece, our Best Man.

God was pleased with our choices, and He was at our wedding ceremony on that day. He gave us showers of blessings, and His presence was richly felt, especially when the congregation sang *I must have the Savior with me*. Merlin is the best thing that ever happened to me. I have not seen or met a better gentleman on planet earth. You do not have to take my word for it. If you know him, you will agree. To the singles—he has two (2) younger brothers who are not free, but they are single, I'm not sure about engagement.

Our Honeymoon

This is one aspect of my life that I wish I could re-live. Our honeymoon was a disaster. My new husband took me to the house we would be living in with my mother-in-law in the guest room, and me a virgin with my period. Well, I thank my period up to this day for coming two days before our wedding, for I was terribly frightened to meet my husband in that phase of our relationship. I needed a period to relax me. Oh blessed period, I thank you. I feel that you may leave me now and pause! And you may do it in the form of the MEN, O PAUSE!

Our Children

After almost four (4) years of marriage, I became seriously concerned that I was unable to conceive. My gynecologist told me that nothing was wrong, but it was just a matter of time. I prayed earnestly, fasted, reminded the Lord how I loved children, and to confirm this, I also reminded him how the Junior Choir came to my house for rehearsal every Saturday. I also told Him that I preferred to die, than to live a life without children of my own. Something close to what Rachel told Jacob in the Bible (Gen.30vs1).

My doctor sent me for a DNC. I think this was a minor operation during which carbon dioxide was blown through the fallopian tubes to clear them from any obstruction, and to ensure that there were no blockages. My mother during that same time, mixed some spices in some red wine, which was, she said, to warm up my tummy, and to remove any lining cold that may be there, preventing conception. I do not know which one the Lord used, but the following month I conceived. When I missed my first period, I was elated. I rushed to the doctor's office but it was too early to tell. I waited impatiently the following month, and as expected, the period did not come.

Charlene Morella Reece

I visited the doctor again and the pregnancy was confirmed. I was so happy that I did not hear a word the doctor uttered after the good news. The few yards from the doctor's office to my husband who was eagerly waiting in the car, seemed to be an eternity. When I got close enough I shouted, "We did it Myrl, we did it, Charlene or Kirwin is here!" I had those names from Secondary School. Kirwin was changed to Darwin when a lady in our church named her little boy Kirwin. From that time onwards I prayed, Lord let the child be normal, pretty or handsome, ten fingers and ten toes, have velvet skin, brilliant and love the Lord. God answered all those prayers when He gave us Charlene.

On March 13th 1980, Charlene Morella Reece was born. She was an awesome sight to behold. God gave us more than we bargained for. She was a beauty. She weighed eight pounds, five and three quarter ounces, fair-skinned, with blue eyes, yes blue eyes (that changed to brown later). She was bald, I forgot to pray for long hair! Charlene was altogether beautiful, and was something to admire. God truly gives good gifts to His children. I really love this girl. When Charlene was four (4) years old, she looked at me once and said, "Mummy, I love you, but I prefer Daddy." That hurt me a bit, but I was happy. She has said on numerous occasions that she wants to marry a man just like her father. That makes me feel very good. I guess her father feels even better.

Darwin Da Costa Reece

Darwin Da Costa Reece was born over three (3) years later, and he weighed nine pounds. My beloved son was brown skinned, smooth and a flat nose (typical of the Reeces). As he laid on the hospital bed, a woman passed and exclaimed, "Bon Dieu, sa se un boef!!" ("Good God, this is a cow!!"). My son is now tall, dark and handsome, very affectionate, and performs well at school. Now that he is an adult, he is taller than his father. Darwin is a lot like me. He loves children, and elderly folks too, and is very generous. He likes to spend money also, and from a child he told his friends that his family is rich. Today, he still believes that we are a rich family.

After Darwin's birth, the placenta refused to come out of my body and was receding. I had to be taken to theatre to get it out. Once again, God spared my life. I was told that I was in great danger, since I had given birth the night before, and still had the placenta inside of me for over eight hours. Darwin adores me, and I feel very proud of him.

The Closeness of my pair

My two (2) biological children are close. One can hardly wedge anything between them. They love each other immensely from early childhood. I have a very unique pair, and they share many secrets. I have told them that I do not need to know all—just some. I tell them often that I trust them. I have told them to be honest with their father and me, and if a story is out on them, we will believe their side of it. So far, their father and I have not had problems. My children are the best; I have not seen or come across a better pair. I know that yours are the best, too and I have no quarrel with that. They have two (2) friends from cradle days: Emerly and Teddyson. They sing together, go out often and are very close. Their dream is to manage their own musical studio. They sing very well, and form one of the best groups around town. Both Charlene and Darwin at present are overseas attending higher institutions of learning.

Jason Levi Leon

Jason joined our family when he was thirteen (13) months old. His mother left him with a neighbor and said to her that she was going to the city to do some shopping, and would be back. It is now over nineteen years and she is still shopping. Her money has not run short yet. She boarded a plane and went to St. Marten. She returned approximately nine (9) years later. Jason, however, is happy with us, and although he could be extremely mischievous, he is our special child, and we love him. Jason has said that he does not mind going to see his three (3) sisters, but he will never stay in St. Marten. We are earnestly praying for his conversion. Jason is hard working, affectionate and sometimes brought me flowers after school. He has no doubt that we love him.

Most of the time, when Jason was little he would come from school with three or more buttons off his shirt, or sometimes all five off. Somebody always pulled him hard, or he was playing a rough game with his friends. He would sometimes come from school with his clothes extremely dirty. When he does his mischievous things, his response is, "Because I wanted to do it." In 1991, Jay (as he is affectionately called) took four out of five fishes from Charlene's aquarium, squeezed them to death with a ruler and injured the vertebrae of the fifth one in the water. That one swam crooked from that day on. Its life span was shortened from that day too and it lived just for a few days. His response—"Because I wanted to do it."

When Jason was in a good mood, he would dig up almost all plants around the house and replant them. On one of his planting days, he dug up a plant that my husband planted for me which used to bear a flower once a year. It usually came up for my birthday. I would always hear my husband say, "Your birthday gift is coming up Moy." Well, Jason uprooted the plant one day, put it in a jar of water and said, "Mummy look a flower I bring for you." I cried. I showed him that I appreciated the thought of giving me the flower, but my plant was dead for good. I could not punish him for the good gesture; for he was so happy, and felt that he had done something great. I thanked him and tried to explain that there are some plants he should not interfere with, like that one. The plant never grew up again since the root was taken out. It bore an onion-type kind of root.

Debora Valencia Reece

Debora, my husband's first daughter was born in St. Lucia, but was sent to Barbados to live with my husband's mother until she became an adult. When it was vacation time, we would send Debora a ticket so that she could spend some time with us. She liked it, and sometimes expressed that she wanted to stay. We decided that it was best for her to finish her schooling first, and then return home if she desired. She was seventeen (17) months old when she was taken from her mother and brought to her grand-mother, Merlin's mom. When Debbie was twenty, she made that permanent move. I do not believe that my mother-in-law ever forgave us for allowing her to come and live with us, but this was what Debora wanted. Debora has never been rude (if she was, she would not have been at our house). She is helpful and very quiet, too quiet sometimes. She is a gift from God. She fell in love with one of our best church guys, Shawn. She too, had verbalized that she wanted to marry a man just like her dad.

Debora is now married for seven years and shares a brilliant, agile three year old adorable son, JADEN DESHAWN AUGUSTIN. He is everything any grand parent would desire.

Thomas Cyril Reece

Tony is my husband's first son and he is just different. I first fell in love with him when I saw his picture. He was sitting on a stool and barred part of his face like a shy little boy. Well, I was in for a big surprise. Tony is far from being shy. He is bold, inquisitive, too nosey sometimes and, could be a nuisance at times. Tony was performing well at the secondary school he attended until he reached the fifth form. I don't know what happened, but he changed drastically, and was not very interested in his school work, did his final exams in a sloppy manner and, had to be taken to a psychiatrist. Some medication was prescribed for Tony and to this day, he behaves differently.

We are praying that God will really touch him, and bring him to his real senses, so that he can be the very intelligent person that he has proven to be, and live a productive life. We know that God is good and awesome enough to grant us that desire. Meanwhile, Tony is around, and is employed. However, he is 'un par with things', and proves time and time again that he has what it takes to be a very intelligent person.

CHAPTER FOUR

DEPRESSION, THE KILLER—GOD, THE DELIVERER

December 26th 1991 marked the first day in seven months and nine days in which I would suffer a bout of depression. It was also the first day in which I would suffer from insomnia for the same length of time. I suffered from this condition for that long, and it was as if I was living in hell. At that time, my body was extremely stressed from overwork, and I was also pursuing a course in Public Administration. On that specific night, I tossed and turned without a wink. I felt miserable while all types of thoughts invaded my mind. My brother, who was then a drug addict, was acting up and misbehaving on the streets of Castries. He was engaging in all types of undesirable behavior, and people were calling our house complaining. I just could not take it anymore. Since I was studying, I woke up at three every morning, and did some work. I was getting good grades.

At the same time, we were purchasing a new home, and needed a deposit of fifty thousand dollars ($50,000.00). I did not have the money so my dear father lent it to me, after we agreed that after our first house was sold, the money would be returned.

At that time, I was also involved in another major project. A group of us decided to renovate our pastor's house while he was away on vacation for two weeks. We did a lot of work at nights, and when they returned it was a pleasant surprise. All seemed to be sailing smoothly. My body began speaking to me, but I did not take heed. I continued to study amidst the hurdles in my life. I ignored all warning signals, and continued my daily routine.

At that time, I was also a member of the Church Council, member of the Church Board, General Secretary of the Church Board, Superintendent of the Sunday School, one of the church janitors, member of the Board of the Inter-School and College Christian Fellowship (ISCCF), Treasurer of the National Insurance Sports and Social Club, (NISSC), Public and Administrative student, mother, wife, lover.

Now when I look back, I say to myself, "bionic lady, you were absolutely crazy!!" Yes, indeed I was, and I suffered the consequences. I continued to have sleepless nights, and began to worry about my state of health. Some severe headaches also started, and I seemed helpless. Around that same time, our proposal for the loan to purchase the house was before the bankers for approval, and all seemed clear. I had been given the keys to the house, and had shown it to most of my friends. The price for the house was two hundred and thirty thousand East Caribbean dollars ($230,000.00), but I was getting it for two hundred and ten thousand dollars ($210,000.00) family price, since the owner was my cousin.

My father who was an old contractor said that it was good and that I should buy it. The children had seen their rooms and were very excited. Our 'stuff' was in barrels waiting to be transported, and we were just waiting for the bank's approval. Whilst we were eagerly waiting, a call came from my cousin's wife informing me that the house was sold to a couple who came from England. I could not believe it at first, and thought that was a big joke. The couple came, saw the house, liked it and paid two hundred and thirty thousand dollars for it.

I felt betrayed, and like a big fool with the keys in my hands. I cried and did not know how to break the news to my children. I called my sister-in-law who consoled me by saying that God had something bigger and better. I have seen this come to pass. The house which we now live in is indeed bigger and better. To God be the glory. I really felt hurt, and the children were very disappointed. I returned the keys with a heavy heart and began looking for another house, but gave up the search after a few days. My husband was not very vocal at that time, but he reminded me that *'all things work together for good, to them that love the Lord, to them that are the called according to His purpose'* **(Romans 8:28).** He also encouraged me by telling me to *wait on the Lord, be of good courage, and He shall strengthen your heart, wait I say on the Lord.* (Psalm 27:14).

I was upset and angry, but my husband though hurting too, was as cool as a cucumber. I returned my father's fifty thousand dollars ($50,000.00). A few of my friends encouraged me to keep it, and told me that it would be for the house that he never built for my sister and I. "After all," they continued, "He is a contractor, and he is your father, so no big deal, that would not be stealing." Some of the things they were saying made sense to me, but I was not comfortable with it. I decided to call my father. I told him that I was returning the money, but my father did not have a clue as to what I tried to explain to him. He completely forgot. He was suffering from amnesia. I called my sister-in-law again, and she encouraged me to return the money. I did and felt peaceful after that. Since then, my husband and I by God's grace have worked hard, and now own three (3) properties. Truly, God is really awesome.

After losing that house, my condition worsened. My body at that time was extremely stressed out, I lost my appetite and began to lose weight very rapidly. I continued to study, despite my sleepless nights, although my ability to concentrate and retain was deteriorating. I visited doctors, drank medicine, but my condition worsened. By the middle of January 1992, my doctor advised me to give up the course, since I was so stressed out.

Studying in that mental state could have caused serious implications. It was very difficult for me to drop the course. I had applied for it for many years, was looking forward to pass it with 'flying colours', was one of the few chosen from the many who applied, and now I had to give up the course. That devastated me. I felt like a big failure. So far I was doing fine with my assignments, and was looking forward to passing my exams for the first semester. I felt like a nobody. I got angry, really angry, even at God. The devil began to devote much of his busy time to me. I also began to listen to all the things that he had to say. Some of the things included that I was a nobody, I had not achieved anything in this life, and that my children would not amount to anything. Charlene was then in Form One (1), Darwin was in Standard One (1), and Jason was in Stage One (1).

He said to me that, that was the furthest they would reach with their education. All three of them would not go further than 'the Ones'. The devil continued by saying that my family would be separated, and that I would go crazy. He accused me of being a hypocrite, and told me that I would also lose my job. He said that I would eventually die. I believed almost everything that he said. In the midst of all this, however, I made up my mind to fight because I had proven God too many times before.

I was prepared to fight for my position in Christ, fight for my precious family and my sanity. I would gird up my loins to fight until I won this battle. God had been too good to me for me to give up easily. I had been delivered from too much trouble before, and seeing that the devil uses the same tricks and tactics because he has nothing new, I started to fight and decided not to give up until I had won the battle. I fought even though I did not see myself winning. I knew that *the race was not for the swift, the battle was not for the strong, but to those that endured to the end* (Eccl. 9:11). I was prepared to die fighting.

At one point in time, it appeared as if the more I fought, the more things worsened. But I kept on fighting. The fight was a spiritual battle, and I knew that I would not always see physical evidence of victory. I tried hard, and again I seemed to be sinking deeper into misery and the depression. The devil said, "SUICIDE", but I knew that was not the answer. He showed me several easy ways in which I could commit the act, and exit from planet earth. Jump from a tall building in the United States; and if you have been there or seen pictures of the place, you would agree that there are some real tall skyscrapers. He also said that it would be easy to slit my throat with a sharp object, drink a poisonous substance, drink an overdose of sleeping pills or drive down a precipice. Thank God, Satan lost again.

My Trip to Barbados

In June of 1992, my sister-in-law accompanied me on a trip to Barbados to see a psychiatrist. Her husband paid all the expenses. That trip was useless. I met a psychiatrist who was not sensitive at all, and who made me feel worse. She prescribed Amitryptylline, and asked me to take it at nights. I took two (2) pills on the first night following the visit to her office, and at about 9:00 p.m. fell asleep. At about midnight, I dreamt that a hearse was coming in the gap to my mother-in-law's house, and was coming for me. I jumped out of bed, and to my amazement, the two pills that I thought I had swallowed were in my mouth. I quickly ran to the bathroom and spewed them out. The hearse never arrived and I was relieved. I never took those pills again and never returned to that psychiatrist because in my opinion, she was of no use.

My Trip to the USA

My next move was to the USA. I traveled alone. My children usually cried whenever I was traveling. They would cry and ask to either come with me or ask me not to go. Not this time. Nobody cried. They were waving me heartily as though they knew that I would return better. I believe my husband spoke to them. As my family waved me, the devil said to me, "Wave them, wave them, this is the last time you are going to see them." I wore a black and white dress to travel and on the way, he said, "You have on the appropriate dress for the funeral, they are going to bury you in that dress." I said to God, "God, if I do not get better, and I have to return the same way that I am going, or worse, I do not want to come back alive, but in a box."

On my way to America, I prayed, "Lord, please lead me to the right psychiatrist, let him/her prescribe the right medicine, and you give me the cure." God heard and answered that prayer. God led me to a doctor who 'knew his stuff'. From the on start, he did the right thing. He questioned me until I was tired. By the time he was finished, he had a book of about twenty pages. The only question I did not answer truthfully was whether I was suicidal. I did not want the doctor to believe that I was capable of taking my life. To me that bit of information was too personal (although he must have sensed that I was lying).

The doctor said that Prosac was fairly new on the market and that it had worked wonders for many people. He said that he could not guarantee that it would cure me, but he would let me use it to see what would happen. I felt like an experiment. When I left the doctor's office, I continued to pray. I said, "Lord, let the Prosac work for me."

At that time, I was instructed to take one Prosac twice a day, and a sleeping pill at nights. I also drank Ensure, a nutritious drink three times a day, in addition to my three meals. In no time, I was beginning to put on weight and look good. I visited the psychiatrist three times, over a three-week period. I had to be transported by my brother-in-law (my sister's husband) to my other brother-in-law's house (my husband's brother).

Doctor Reece, (my brother-in-law's wife) would then transport me to the psychiatrist in the evening. Every time I entered their home in Long Island, I would quickly run to the guest room and go beneath the covers and just stay there. The only time I got up was when I became hungry. I would run to the kitchen downstairs, eat, and run back beneath the covers. I was alone, and that was the pattern I followed during the first two visits.

The desire to commit suicide was still there. The devil tempted me to drink the sleeping pills and, 'call that George' but I could not do it. This scripture always came to memory, "***Greater is He that is in me, than he that is in the world***" (John 4:4). I prayed and tried my best to believe God, but there were times when I felt helpless and hopeless. The enemy accused me of being a hypocrite all my life, and that God was disappointed in me. I still felt that my world was closing in, and that it was just a matter of time before everything exploded. I found myself talking in a negative manner. When I was being transported to my brother-in-law's house, I would complain and say things like, "I am fed up with this thing . . . it was time for this foolishness to be over . . . God has forgotten me . . . I'd rather be dead than to be in this state I got myself into this mess . . . enough is enough . . . how much more can someone take . . . I'm sick and tired of being sick and tired."

God the Deliverer

Something happened during the third visit. My brother-in-law observed it and told my sister. I was speaking positively. When I arrived at the house, I immediately ran to the room and headed for the covers as usual. I took a sleeping pill. This was not customary because I usually took it at nights. I was awakened by the sound of chiming church bells; there was a church nearby. All of a sudden, I felt like looking outside. I got up immediately, and looked out of the bedroom window. When I drew the curtains, I began to admire the beauty of nature. I felt an urge to go outside. There was a very large yard. I rushed to the yard and sat on a swing, and as I swung, it seemed that nature began to unfold.

I noticed the greenness of the grass; I heard the chirping of the birds; I looked up into the sky and the feeling was ethereal. I suddenly had the urge to go shopping. I wanted my family close to me and I desired my husband intimately. I desperately needed companionship. I ran inside the house and took pen and paper. I wrote all the positive feelings that I was experiencing, and feelings that I had not experienced for seven (7) months and nine (9) days. "My God," I shouted, "is this thing real?" You mean that I can really live again? my God, I thank You." I was so excited, that I could hardly sit. I could hardly wait for someone to come home, to break the news to them. I felt like running all over the neighborhood, but I knew that would be crazy. I was elated. My brother-in-law's wife was the first to come home. She noticed that I was out of bed and smiling. She was very happy for me. I could hardly wait to see the doctor. I felt like skipping and dancing. This healing I thought deserved a celebration. I had to contain myself.

The afternoon came and I was eager to see the doctor. At one glance, the doctor observed that something had happened. When he inquired, I attributed the healing to God. "Well," he said, "it must be some God or something, but something did happen." From that day onwards, I was happy. I had prayed with Angel, a good friend the day before, for over two hours for my healing. I had also planted a seed. I called Richard Roberts Ministry and told them that the following day was my husband's birthday, and if there is one gift I would like to give him is to tell him that 'all is well', and really mean it.

Someone prayed for me over the telephone, and I felt better. God did answer those prayers, and for this I am very grateful. That made me love God more. I realized, however, that the depressed feelings were resurfacing after two days. I prayed, went out shopping, and the bad feelings left. The following day was a good one. Two (2) days later, I felt that I was down in the deeps. When I realized what was happening, I took a stand against the devil. I went to the bathroom and had it out with 'Old Slew Foot'. I told him that he was a dirty stinking liar and that he would not succeed with what he was trying to do. I reminded him of the proverb, 'He who laughs last, laughs the best', and told him that he had his laugh, and that it was my turn to laugh. I told him that I had something for him, which was a kick. I literally kicked him. "Take this devil," I shouted. I also stamped on him, crushed his head, and said, "case closed!!" I never had a bad day again. To God be the glory, truly He is a faithful God.

Veronica, one of my good friends who resides in the USA, came to see me on one of my bad days. She came to take me to the Bronx Zoo, but I did not want to go. She actually forced me to leave the house. Surprisingly I enjoyed it. Vay Vay (her nickname) said to me, "Moy, I do not know if this is possible, but if you do not have sufficient faith to believe God for your healing, I will believe God for you." I appreciate this statement up to this day. By early September, I returned to St. Lucia and was 'flying high'. I had to be slowed down with Lithium to stabilize me. I then made a complete turn around. I was back at work on March 3rd 1993. I resumed some duties in church and resigned from some. I was driving fast, eating a lot, and spending a lot of money. I purchased a deep freezer and a big refrigerator in one day. I spent eleven thousand dollars ($11,000.00) in one month, and could hardly account for some other monies that were spent. I did things that made me marvel that I actually did them, but God was there to bring me out of there safely. Thank God I am sane and ticking.

After The Depression

I prayed and read the word, but in a shallow manner. I was too busy, too hyperactive, caring for, and sharing with others. As soon as my cupboards were empty, I filled them up again. After all the money was gone, over twenty thousand dollars ($20,000.00), the friends surprising stayed, unlike the Prodigal Son.

I do not know why God allowed my family to go through this rough period, but we all say to Him be all the glory that will come out of it. My husband at that time was married to me for fifteen (15) years, my daughter was eleven (11), my son was tight (8), Jason was five (5) and Debora was an adult. We stuck together through thick and thin. We held on even when the church folks had given up on us and were tired of me being ill. Thank God that He was there all the time. Sometimes we needed human shoulders to lean on, but almost everyone was too busy with their own affairs. It appeared then that they did not care about us.

There is a recitation that my husband gave me when I was seventeen and courting. I would like to share it with you. It was a great source of strength to me during my illness, and has blessed many. It is entitled, ***Our Matchless Christ***.

OUR MATCHLESS CHRIST

To many, Jesus Christ is only a grand subject for a painting, a heroic theme for a pen, a beautiful form for a statue or a thought for a song. But to those who have heard His voice, who have felt His pardon, and who have received His benediction, He is music, warmth, light, joy, hope and salvation.

A friend who never forsakes, who lifts us when others try to push us down. We cannot wear Him out. We pile on Him all our griefs and troubles. He is always ready to lift us, He is always ready to help us. He addresses us with the same love, He beams upon us with the same smile, He pities us with the same compassion. There is no name like His. It is more inspiring than Caesar's, more musical than Beethoven's, more patient than Lincoln's. The name of Jesus throbs with all life, weeps with all pathos, groans with all pains, stoops with all love. Its breath is laden with perfume.

Who like Jesus can pity a homeless orphan? Who like Jesus can welcome a prodigal back home? Who like Jesus can make a drunkard sober? Who like Jesus can illuminate a cemetery ploughed with graves? Who like Jesus can make a queen unto God out of a lost woman on the streets? Who like Jesus can catch the tears of human sorrow in His bowl? Who like Jesus can kiss away our sorrows?

I struggle for a metaphor with which to express Jesus. He is not like the bursting forth of an orchestra, that is too loud, and it may be out of tune. He is not like the sea when lashed into a rage by a storm, that is too boisterous, He is not like the mountain wreathed in lightening, canopied with snow, that is too solitary and remote.—HE IS THE LILY OF

THE VALLEY, THE ROSE OF SHARON, A GALE OF SPICES FROM

HEAVEN.

By Billy Sunday

To God Be The Glory

To God be the glory. I am alive today only by the grace of The Almighty God. After seven months and nine days of depression, I can stand and say to God be the glory for all that I went through. Let Him be praised. I can now see the reasons why He allowed me to be depressed for that amount of time. It is for His glorification. If I had to be taken there again, as long as the Lord is going with me, I am willing and ready to go. The good Lord rescued me just in time and I believe it is because He has a plan and purpose for my life.

If there are any depressed persons reading this book, (although depressed persons hardly read), please remember that you are not alone. There are many people like you, and there is a God who can and who is willing to bring you out of that state. You need to believe this. If you have forgotten all that you have read so far in this book, I want you to remember this:

1) *You are not depressed because of some sin that you have committed.*
2) *God has not deserted you.*
3) *There is hope for you.*
4) *You can be cured (please believe this).*
5) *Behind every black cloud there is a silver lining.*
6) *Stay tuned to God.*
7) *Pray without ceasing. Do it even when you don't feel like it. If you can't pray, groan, the Holy Spirit will interpret for you.*
8) *Read, study and ponder on God's word even when you don't care to. There is life in the word of God.*
9) *If you feel mocked when you pray, just pray more. This is a trick of the enemy.*
10) *Plant a seed for your healing.*
11) *Give thanks, yes you read correctly, give thanks for your healing. God is carrying you even if you can't feel or see Him. Stop looking down, and begin to look up.*
12) *Get one or two persons to pray and believe with you.*
13) *Close your eyes and ears to the dirty and stinking prompting of the devil.*
14) *Claim your miracle even when there are doubts in your mind.*

Again I say, pray. If you find time to pray, God has the time to listen. HELP IS ON THE WAY!!

CHAPTER FIVE

THE BIG 'C', CANCER

A few weeks before I observed a small lump in my right breast, I had a frightening dream. That dream may have been a signal of a very disturbing and challenging time for me. I woke up from the dream, trembling and with my heart palpitating. I quickly woke up my husband, and sat on the bed relating the dream to him as vividly as I could remember. We prayed about it soon afterwards.

The Dream

I was with a group of women outside the Golden Hope Hospital (a mental institution). We had bibles in our hands so it seemed that we had either ended a religious meeting, or some ministry to the sick folks at that institution.

We gathered outside the main entrance to the ward of the male patients conversing. We were then alerted by a sharp shrieking noise. When I looked in the direction of the main door which was ajar, I saw this witch-like creature dressed in black with a hat (one with a peak), bulging fiery eyes, a long pointed nose, long claws for fingernails and she was flying above the heads of the patients and making her way outside the door.

The witch then made a left turn towards us. As she swerved, she seemed to be directing her flight or her attention towards me. At that time, I became terribly frightened, and turned to run away from the creature. Whilst I was running away from her, I heard a desperate and angry voice. It was Merlin's. He was nowhere in the group, and at that point was not in the dream, but I heard him shouting, "Morella, turn around and face the woman!!"

I turned immediately, and as I did so, the witch clawed my face from below my eyes and down my neck stopping on my chest. I quickly lifted her up as high as I could, threw her down and broke her back. It was at that point that I jumped from my sleep.

I went to church the following day, and related the dream to the congregation. I remembered saying on the pulpit, "I do not know what the dream means, but whatever it is, I am willing to go through it as long as the Lord goes with me."

A few weeks after that dream, July 1997, I observed a small, yet unusual swelling on my right breast one day while undressing for a shower. I drew closer to the mirror to examine the swelling. Since I had recently joined the gym, I attributed the swelling to exercise. I recalled feeling a sting in that same area one morning while doing some stretches on a machine at the gym. It felt like the type of sting and popping that one experiences when a rubber band bursts. That is how I can describe the sting in the same area where the lump was eventually found. In my mind, I planned to get the swelling examined by a doctor soon after it was observed. I procrastinated of course, and it was while having dinner one night with my family, that I felt two stings in the same spot. They felt as though someone had pricked me twice with a needle. The stings were so sharp that they jolted my body. I immediately told my family what I had just experienced. Well, the next day I was standing outside the door of the St Lucia Cancer Society, waiting for the place to be opened. I was not taking any more chances. The swelling was examined by a doctor, but at that point it was too early to tell whether there was a lump. I was sent for a mammogram. One day after completing my inspectorate duties and returned to the office, I found a note on my desk which read 'Please see Doctor Beaubrun at the Cancer Society'.

My heart missed two beats. My mind was in a muddle. If it was not serious, she would not send for me. My mind told me that there was a lump, and that it was malignant. The result was abnormal. The X-ray showed the swelling as a cloud. Perhaps it was too early to tell. I asked the doctor what was the next step. She advised that since a lump was not ruled out, I had a choice to wait for a few weeks, and then have another mammogram. However, she said that she was not prepared to take any chances, and that I should return within four to six weeks. When I sensed the seriousness in her voice, I said to the doctor, "Doctor, if you can cut me today, and tell me what is in my breast, I am willing to be cut." When she saw how desperate I was, she sent me for a biopsy. The biopsy was painful, a large needle was inserted into the area, and some stuff was extracted. Two long tears came from my eyes. The doctor, however, was caring and friendly so I tried to relax.

While awaiting the results of the biopsy (over six weeks), I told myself that it could not be cancer. After all, there was no one in my family who had ever been diagnosed with the disease. I was doing all the right things—exercising, eating well, sleeping, recreating and serving God faithfully. What else was there to do? The results came, and again it was abnormal.

My God, I thought, what is happening? I was advised that the next step was surgery. The doctor explained that unless the lump was taken out of the body and tested, one could not tell whether it was cancerous or not. In two days, I was on the operating table. I asked for the soonest possible date. I had computer exams on the same day. I really did not care about that because I felt that my health should be given priority, and that everything else could wait. The surgery was successful. The lump was one and a half centimeters, so it was take out with a small amount of tissue. The doctor explained that, that was the way he would go considering my age, and the size of the lump. I was happy that I did not need a mastectomy, although I would learn to live with it. Better one has one or no breasts than to lose an eye, or an arm. Up to that point, I was optimistic.

I went into surgery positively, hoping that the lump would be benign. I told myself that I could not be the first one in my family history with cancer. No way I thought. I waited impatiently for the result. I told myself no news was good news. I began to prepare for the worse, as I awaited the results. My faith began to dwindle, and the devil began to oppress me. The devil said that the results would be malignant. I felt positive sometimes, but negative at other times.

The results came this time while I was at home having lunch. The phone rang, and the doctor's secretary said that the doctor asked me whether I could come to his office at 3:00 p.m. Well my heart missed three beats this time, and began to palpitate. I did not want to continue eating. I told myself that the results were serious because the doctor would not have asked me to come in. Every time I visited the doctor before, my husband accompanied me, and the doctor was always careful to explain everything to the two of us, and answer all our questions. That afternoon I did not feel for company, I wanted to go for that particular result alone.

I went in to see the doctor, and with all the compassion that a doctor could break the news to a patient, he told me that the lump was cancerous. "Morella," he said, "This is one of the most difficult things for a doctor to say to a patient—the lump is malignant". My first reaction was to look up and exclaim, "O God!" I was disappointed. I became instantly depressed. The doctor said a few things which I did not hear. I remember asking him what next. He said another surgery to check whether the cancer had spread to the lymph nodes. I arranged that to be done as soon as possible. I really needed my husband then. I needed a shoulder to cry on.

I left the doctor's office and as soon as I reached outside of Tapion Hospital, the tears were streaming down my cheeks. "Why God, Why?" I asked. "Why me?" I never believed that the lump could be cancerous, although I knew that there was a possibility. I felt that I was too good to be afflicted with that plague. Was it something I had done, and God was punishing me I thought. I was confused. I felt betrayed by God. After all, He should have allowed the cancer to afflict someone else, knowing that I would help them get better, but not me. I did not even feel like driving. The tears felt warm as they streamed down my face uncontrollably.

I went to my office, dropped my bag there, told myself that that was the last time I would be coming to that place and left. The devil told me that I would lose the job sooner or later. Honestly at that point, I did not really care. I headed for my husband's office. I told him that the lump was malignant. His response was similar. "My God," he said. He then asked me a few questions which I answered, and became quiet after this. That quietness lasted for one year and three months. I was, however screaming in God's face. I felt that my world was closing in. My husband and I drove in silence.

When I got home, I prepared for computer classes. I do not know why I went. I guess I wanted to do something which would distract me from the one thing foremost on my mind. My husband drove me to classes, and came back for me. Exam was two days away. I visualized myself dying. The student next to me kept teasing me due to my quietness. I was never quiet at classes. Mandy kept nudging me, asking me to say something. We always joked and chatted at classes and she missed that. It was easy for me to tell her of my present state because I had already told her that I was awaiting the result of the cancer test. She had given me some hope when she told me that she had had three lumps taken out from her breasts and they were all benign. She kept quiet when I broke the sad news to her. I thought that she felt sorry for me and did not know what to say.

We drove in silence on our way home. When my husband was about a quarter mile away from home, I told him that I was unable to go home, and that he should take me somewhere. I began crying aloud. He enquired as to where I wanted to go. I told him to just take me somewhere. By then I was screaming hysterically. The windows of the vehicle were closed, and as I screamed, I thought that I would have passed out (died).

My husband took me to the beach near the George Charles Airport. I cried bitterly. I screamed at God asking Him, "Why?" I screamed and kept saying, "No", all of the time. After I got weak, and had little energy left, I stopped. We went home. The next hurdle was to tell the children. I wanted to spare them the trauma, the hurt. We could not tell them. We called Debora into our bedroom and told her. Two long tears ran down her cheeks. We never told the others, they heard it from other sources.

The Second Surgery

The second surgery was scheduled as soon as it was possible. Under my right arm was cut and cleared. After some checks were done, no malignant cells were found, and that meant that the cancer had not spread to the lymph nodes. The doctors were elated, but I was so depressed at that time, it really did not matter whether the cancer had spread or was localized. In fact, I believed that it had already spread, and that it was just a matter of time before I die. I was discharged from the hospital after two days.

Radiotherapy

A few weeks after leaving Tapion Hospital, I had to undergo radiotherapy at Queen Elizabeth Hospital in Barbados for six (6) long weeks. During radiotherapy, the patient lies in a room by himself or herself, and machines are hooked up to him or her. Each of my treatments lasted for ten to fifteen minutes. Absolutely no pain is felt, although the area which is being treated is exposed to intense heat. One feels very lonely in the room although he is being monitored by nurses through a glass window outside the room. It was rough. I had to be transported to the hospital five days a week. The doctor's report stated that my 'body tolerated the treatment well'. Amidst all that, the depression continued and I prayed to die but death would not come. During the treatments I lived with my friends, Trevor and Marquitta Simmons. They treated me as family. Trevor drove me to the hospital for the entire six weeks, and I did not hear him complain. He sat in the waiting room everyday like a husband would wait for his wife. That is what I call friendship. ***Thank you Trev and Marquita, Lexi and Mark. May the Omnipotent One bless all of you unconditionally. You are four precious people, and I appreciate and cherish our friendship.***

After six weeks of radiotherapy, I looked in the mirror and was horrified at the picture that I saw. Part of my body looked charred. The area on the right side of my chest which was treated, the right side of my neck, my right ear, and the right side of my back were really black. I hated the person looking back at me in the mirror. I hated myself.

However, amidst all of this, I still had reason to give thanks. There was a fifteen-year old teenager being treated who had cancer behind her nose, and after the radiotherapy treatment, her entire face was charred. She told me that her sense of taste and smell were gone, and that God alone knew what else would be affected. I had lived half of my life already, but she had just begun hers. I felt very sorry for her.

During the entire six weeks of treatment, I sat in the waiting room with other cancer patients, and wondered who would die first. A few of them looked dilapidated. Some were thin and pale. Most of them had lost their hair and were either bald, or wearing a wig. One could easily tell by the way their clothes fit that some had lost weight. There was a dreary look on their faces as they chatted among themselves on the way the treatment affected the quality of their lives. I listened everyday, and seldom participated in their conversations. My mind was too busy wondering who would die before me.

I also moaned about the fact that there was no support group to help us cope. Nobody seemed to care that our bodies were being burnt by all that radiation. There was no one with whom we could share our pain, our fears. We needed advice on how to treat our thinning hair, deal with the loss of weight and skin discoloration. However, it seemed that everybody was in their own little world, whilst we were tagging behind them. That hurt badly.

At the end of the six weeks, I was thankful that I was returning home to my family. A family that loved me just as I was. During the time that I was in Barbados, my husband had visited me once. I was comforted by the fact that he would be at the airport waiting to welcome me home. I had absolutely no doubt that he would have accepted me—my partly-charred skinny body.

On my arrival, Merlin welcomed me with open arms, and a broad smile which said everything to me. His first words were, "Sweetheart, you're looking good." I felt his deep warmth as he held me, and did not let the fact that I looked terrible doubt how he really felt about me.

Chemotherapy

After radiotherapy, my body had to undergo the rigors of chemotherapy for six months. The drugs were administered intravenously once a month. By that time, I had lost a considerable amount of weight, and my self esteem had dropped to near zero. I looked in the mirror often, and did not like the person looking back at me. I looked awful, and wished everyday that I would just die.

I was told by the doctor that the drugs which were inserted in the drip was poison which would kill any cancer cells that may be found, and in the process it would also kill thousands of normal cells. This is the reason why most cancer patients are weak for hours, or sometimes days after the chemotherapy treatment. Some people become nauseous and even vomit during the treatments, but I remained calm. I just felt a bit weak afterwards, and would head for my bed. Cancer patients have to eat well in order to replace those normal cells that are destroyed. A cell count has to be done before every treatment. If the result is unsatisfactory, the doctor sends the patient at home and he or she is advised on the right foods to eat, to build up the count.

My doctor told me that I was doing very well, and tried to make me feel better. I was at work sometimes, and at home sometimes. Thank God for my supervisors, who believed in me more than I believed in myself. They comforted me and said that after I was through with the treatments, I would do much better. They were right, but I did not believe it. My services could have been terminated, or I could have been sent home, and retired on medical grounds, but I thank God that that was not done. I stayed away from work for many days, and it seemed that everybody understood. I struggled and struggled, and fought the depression, but I did not seem to be making much progress. Many people were concerned. Church folks, work folks, neighbors, my family, even some of my enemies.

I seemed to be getting worse, although my entire body was scanned in Barbados after Radiotherapy and no malignant cells were found. The devil oppressed my mind and told me that the cancer had spread all through my body and even my brain was plagued with cancer cells. I included my brain because my mental faculties were not working properly, and I could hardly concentrate. I was not sleeping, and that was the real cause, but I believed at that time that it was the cancer. I watched people on the streets, at church, and wished that I was in their place. I wanted to be anyone, but Morella.

I continued to cry silently, and prayed earnestly that I would die in my sleep every night, but that never became a reality. Thoughts of suicide clouded my mind, but I did not share them with anyone. I watched my children in a pitiful manner. The devil showed me that they were failing and dying—no energy, no desire to eat, and my heart hurt every time I watched them. All three of them failed their exams, and that had never occurred in our family, that was not the norm. That brought me deeper into the depression, and I cried to God and showed Him what the devil was doing to my children, in order to get at me. It appeared that God just ignored me and did not care. The devil told me that my children would be part of the statistics of school dropouts, and I believed it.

I continued to worry and lose weight. Prior to the cancer diagnosis, I weighed one hundred and fifty-five pounds (155). While I was sick, I was reduced to one hundred and twenty pounds (120). My mirrors told me that I looked terrible; my clothes were hanging on me like they would hang from a hanger. My eyes were sunken, and my shoulders were drooping. My hair was thinning, and I did not have the desire to go to the hairdresser. I only wanted to die.

Even in that state, my husband would say to me that I looked good, and that it was only a matter of time for me to put on the weight that I had lost, and would look like the Morella he knew. He kept encouraging me by saying that after the chemotherapy, he would have his wife back. He had much more faith than me. My children got closer to me, and flooded me with hugs and kisses, to make me feel better, they thought, but the closer they got to me, the more I saw them dying.

There is a young hungry-looking chap that appears on the television on one of the religious programs which makes appeals on behalf of hungry children in Africa. He looked like my son, and I would picture Darwin like that, and the devil said that he would become like that since he had no desire to eat.

I desired to be alone most of the time. I stayed in the bedroom and watched mostly religious programs on television. I enjoyed it sometimes. At times, I felt that God cared and was there, but most of the time, I thought that He did not care, since I had committed a 'grievous sin', and was being punished for it (although I could not point my finger on the sin), and because of that, He had withdrawn His presence. Many Christians who heard that I was sick came to pray for me. They came, and while they prayed I even questioned the sincerity of their prayers. I felt that they were wasting their time, although I knew that 'prayer changes things'. I felt hopeless. Sometimes I detested their visits. When someone is depressed, he or she does not appreciate company, whether the purpose of the visit is to pray, or play. One often loses valuable friends during depression, although I feel that if the friends are genuine, they would stay.

Money and Depression

I am a spender, but when I am depressed, I have no use for money. I just cannot handle it (this is the only time my husband gets his peace). When the depression is over, I spend!!! When the depression is on, I do not like to go shopping for fear that people would see me. I just want to stay at home. My husband insisted that I go to the supermarket, even if it was once a month. Even that was strenuous. I dragged myself to the supermarket and dragged myself out. Nothing at the supermarket seemed to make any sense.

I saw nothing to purchase, as though it was a waste of time to even shop. I would walk up and down the aisles, and if the children and my husband were not there, I was sure that I would leave with hardly anything. I was just sick and tired of being sick and tired. One night I went to bed and said to God, "Enough is enough, and if you do not get me out of whatever I was going through, I would help myself."

CHAPTER SIX

I BEAR THE MARKS

It was October 26th 1998, the day after Jounen Kweyol, (Creole Day) when a few members of staff as is customary after an event, gathered in pockets to discuss highlights of the day. I got to work early. The pockets were already forming, and there was a lot of laughter. I remember sitting in my seat and saying to God. "God hear them, are you listening? Hear how happy they sound. All of them must have slept last night. God, most of them are not Christians, I am one, and I feel so miserable. God are you there, God do you care? My God, where are you? God if I was not sick, you know I would be leading that conversation. My God do something." I screamed silently. I got up from my chair, said to my supervisor that I was going out, and I silently told myself that I would never return to that office again. All I thought of doing at that point was to take my life.

"My God", I continued to cry, "I don't want to go to hell, and you know how afraid I am of hell, please help me. My God please open a door for me. What about my husband, what about my children? What about the church which my husband pastors? My God I cannot do this, what will the church folks say? What will my enemies say? What about my testimony?" I continued to question God, but it seemed the deeper the agony, the more He ignored me. I arrived at home at about 8:45 a.m. I was in torment, thoughts were racing in my mind. I began to think and even picture my biological family and others, after I had committed the act.

I could not stand the thoughts. My daughter was at home, she had completed her tertiary education, and was awaiting calls for interviews from the numerous applications that she had sent out. She was watching television, and did not have a clue as to what I was contemplating. I went to my bathroom and continued to talk to God. "My God," I continued, "I cannot drink poison, I don't seem to have the guts to do it. In fact, I do not even know whether there is any in the house." I opened the cupboard and found something marked poison. It was almost empty. I went downstairs and punctured it with a knife, intending to drink the contents, but it exploded.

Nobody was aware of anything. The noise was not loud enough to raise any suspicions. I returned upstairs, and looked in the cupboard again. I found motor oil. That oil was given to us when our vehicle was purchased five years before. I punctured that, too. I placed it on the top of the cupboard, and was hoping to drink it as soon as I had the courage to do so. My daughter called to ask me whether I was returning to work. I told her that I was not certain. She encouraged me to go but I told her that I was not feeling well.

While the motor oil was near the bathroom sink, I started to pace the floor. I paced it for many hours, and could not drink the contents of the can. I went in and out of the bathroom, speaking to Charlene sometimes. I continued with my pleas to God, "Please Lord, please help me. I'm dying, and you don't seem to care. Please God, I am begging you to do something."

The motor oil was still on the cupboard. The can was rusty. I thought it would have been easy to empty the contents down my throat with a few gulps, but it wasn't easy. I also had two knives, but I did not have the guts then, to stab myself. I finally drank the motor oil, at about 3:30 p.m. It tasted awful, but I drank all of it, one pint. I thought that I would repent after, and all would be well. I did not eat or drink anything for the balance of the day or night, since I wanted the oil to work. It started to boil in my stomach about two hours after, and I felt very uncomfortable. I was also belching a lot.

At approximately 9:00 p.m. I began vomiting. I vomited something pink. I did so about four times. Every time I did, I would clean the bathroom sink, and spray with air freshener to conceal what had happened. Nobody in the house observed what was happening. The last time I vomited, it was tinged with blood. My husband had asked me how my day went, and how I was feeling. I told him that I was not feeling good. He recognized that I was not in a talking mood, and did not prolong the conversation. I bathed and had no dinner. My husband came again and offered me dinner. He also observed that I had not eaten lunch, and questioned me concerning that. He reminded me of the importance of eating right due to the chemotherapy, but I did not respond. I went to bed, but my mind was somewhere else.

I then had diarrhea, was vomiting motor oil, and excreting motor oil. The vomiting stopped the same night, but the diarrhea continued for about three (3) days. I said to God that night, "God, you see that I could do it, however, to prove that you are still there, I would like you to put me to sleep for a few hours." That had not worked for many nights yet I continued to test God with it. He was telling me all the time, "Woman don't put me to the test", but I continued to test Him. I thank Him for His mercy, and

I thank Him that He did not cut me off in my stupidity. "Please God", I pleaded, "just put me to sleep for a few hours and when I wake up, I will say surely God is still there for me." I had not slept properly for a whole year, and one could easily detect that from the way my eyes looked. That night I did not blink my eyes in sleep. I heard every tick of the clock, and every snore in the house. I got angry at God.

My husband and I normally pray at five o'clock every morning and at six o'clock with the whole family. That morning, I got down from the bed at five o'clock, and told my husband that I wanted some time alone. I told God, "God you know that I am afraid to go to hell, and just the thought of going there makes me shiver. Last night, you proved to me that you are not in my corner when you did not help me to sleep. In fact, I am not even sure that you exist anymore. Lord I am trying, but you are not helping me. God, that's it!!!

The Near Tragedy

I rushed to the kitchen and took a knife. I started to slit my wrist. It was cutting me, but the knife was not sharp enough. I started to cut another part of my wrist, but when I could no longer stand the pain I stopped. God stopped me. I was told that if I had gone one centimeter lower, I would have died. I tried to slit my throat with the same knife, but that would not work either. All that time, I was asking God to help me to kill myself. Have you ever heard a more foolish prayer?

I took another knife with a pointed edge. I tried to puncture my esophagus. I leaned over the couch and put all my body weight on the knife. I punctured it in three places, still, I would not die. I heard the sound of the knife as it punctured my gullet, yet I would not stop. It sounded like one cutting through gristle. I said to God, "God just let me collapse on the couch and die. I do not want to end up in hospital for people to come and see me. I will be too embarrassed. Please Lord, just let me die, and let my family find me dead."

My husband came at that point, and asked me if anything was wrong. I used a dark brown velvet bed spread to conceal the blood. I told him that I was just not feeling well. He held me close for a few seconds. "Talk to me Molly," he said, but I had nothing to say. He returned to the bedroom. I leaned on the couch as before and placed the knife in the same wounds that I had punctured earlier, still nothing seemed to happen. I then punctured my chest in two places, in search of my heart, and again nothing happened. I am bionic, I thought. My husband came again. "Come Molly", he said, "please speak to me and tell me what is wrong." Then he observed blood on the floor. "Is that blood? Do you have your period?" I was going to hell, and God did not seem to care so I could tell lies. I said, "Yes I have my period." You have your period, and there is blood on the floor," he said in a puzzled tone. "Come Molly."

My husband drew me close and began to unwrap the bed spread. I will never forget his reaction as long as I live. "O my God! Molly why didn't you tell me. O God! What did you do? Molly why?" He held his head. "What are we going to tell the children, what will happen to our children, what about the church? My God! Molly who should I call?" I asked him to call the Collymores or Josephine, my friend. He said that he would wake up the children, and I asked him not to. He didn't. He called the Collymores, and they came in a flash.

As soon as my brother saw me, he cried out, "O my God! Moy you know that we are there for you and you know that we love you. Why did you do this?" He asked that in a trembling tone. I felt worse than I felt earlier. My husband had wiped the blood from the floor, but my nightgown was soaked in blood. At that point I began to have difficulty in breathing, and I heard blood bubbling from the wounds when I breathed. I changed my clothes and my brother drove me to the hospital. The children were up by that time, and they were all puzzled. No one said a word.

On the way to the hospital, my brother cried, as he reminded me how much they cared. I said nothing much to anyone except that God did not care about me and I am better off dead if He is not on my side. At that point I still prayed that I would die before I reach the hospital. In all this, I still thought that I would have the time to repent and escape hell. Somehow, I felt that God was so merciful, He would forgive me and everything would be alright. I experienced what I did not want—to be at the hospital, and to be visited by friends and all types of people.

Not All Doctors are Doctors

The first nurse was not very pleasant at all, and the first doctor who came into the Casualty Department was worse. Someone had already informed him of my situation and as soon as he saw me he uttered, "So you almost killed yourself, I hope you're feeling better now. So what, will that make the cancer go away?" I did not answer. All I felt was that he deserved a solid kick. As far as I was concerned, he was no doctor. I was upset. I did not need that then. I needed someone who would at least try to understand. I needed some empathy. It became a little more difficult for me to breathe, and when I did, I felt some pain. The blood continued to bubble. When I breathed, the wounds in my chest bubbled. I was never afraid, I do not know why. I was taken to theatre and my wounds were mended.

The two female psychiatrists that I saw at the hospital did not treat me well either. One of them used a tone of voice that made me feel worse. "So you almost killed yourself. What happen, will you try it again?" I answered, "No." That made me upset, too. I was asked to count from one hundred backwards, and keep subtracting seven. I did it easily. I guess they wanted to check my mental faculties. The two of them asked me some other questions. I felt that those doctors were not fit to be in that profession. If my real doctor was like those two, I would have been dead ten times and over. One of them softened up a bit after subsequent visits, and I began to like her.

My Doctor

My doctor is patient, sensitive and very kind. I have not come across a better one. He is never in a hurry, and he makes me feel comfortable. Whether it is a headache or cancer, he is present with the situation, and he knows how to empathize. He is partly responsible for me being on my feet today. When I was sick, going to visit him made me feel better. I have boasted about him with my friends, and they always seem to agree. I really appreciate Dr. Greenidge.

When he saw me at the hospital in all my embarrassment, he said to me, "Morella, you did not do this to yourself. Please hear me, you would never do this to yourself, not the Morella that I know." Boy that made me feel good. He was not judgmental like the others, or even the psychiatrists who, in my opinion, should be the emphatic ones.

Whilst I was being treated for the cancer, and after I was discharged following the suicidal attempts, Dr. Greenidge called my house quite often to find out how I was doing. He followed up on all my calls. He answered all our questions, and was never in a hurry. We felt comfortable with him. That is a doctor!!

I also consider my psychotherapist, Nicole, to be very good at her profession. She is polite, friendly, knows how to make someone relax and 'pour their heart out'. She is young, pretty and very promising. I looked forward to meeting her once a week, and even when I did not need to see her anymore, I felt like visiting her.

Similarities Between my Husband and my Doctor

Both my husband and my doctor are sensitive, kind, patient and empathetic. They both know how to make their presence felt. The words that they use are similar. When I first saw my husband after surgery, he said to me, "Molly you did not do this to yourself. The Morella that I know, love and admire is not capable of doing this. You are depressed, and you had no control of your actions. I love you just the same and more." My husband knows 'what size plaster to put on any sore'. I love him so much. Both my husband and doctor know how to give compliments. Both are attractive, patient and kind.

Surgery Again

I went into surgery and it was successful. I spoke to the doctors, and they all said that it was not an easy task. Both my wrist and throat gave a bit of trouble to repair. And the doctors did such a great job that the wounds are hardly noticeable. I was placed in a ward with three other ladies. They asked me if I was involved in an accident. I said no and did not give any explanation. They were all speaking about their illness. I kept silent since I did not have a very pleasant story to tell. I also felt that if they knew, they might be afraid to be in the same ward as I was.

Floods of people came to see me. Some were genuine, others were curious and some were shocked. My work mates, said to themselves, Not Mrs Reece. But what about her Christian beliefs?" This was revealed to me after I got better. They said that it was so hard to believe because I was someone who was a source of encouragement to so many people. How was it possible for me to do something like that. They were baffled.

One particular Christian lady for whom I have great respect came to see me while many people were around my bed. She went on tip toe, glanced at me quickly, and went out of the door. I felt as though a dagger went through me. That really hurt. "No," I said to myself, "not sister So and So." I felt that she had judged me, and that I had been found guilty. I felt condemned. I told her afterwards, and she apologized. She, however, told me that she was praying for me all of that time. I believed her. I guess she just did not know how to handle that situation.

By the time my story reached town, many people were praying for me. Many of my friends were hiding the information, including my work mates. But I was at the hospital, and they would like people to visit me, but to disclose why I was there was too embarrassing for them. Many of them lied to protect me. *I really understand, and thank you my friends.* What baffled them was how I could do that. After all, I seem to have 'a unique family', a good job, a beautiful house and the few things that would make someone free from headaches. More importantly, I claimed to be a child of God. How? But why? The answer to these questions is—ask the depression.

When one is depressed, he/she is capable of doing anything, and just believe this-case closed. Unless someone has been there, or has been trained to understand, he or she will never understand. I have a good Christian friend who was depressed for over two years, and one day, she took matches, and began to light them under her bed. If you ask her why she did it, she just does not know. She was brought back to reality when she heard someone shout her name from the outside. I believe if God did not do it, He sent an angel to call her name. Thank God.

I was discharged after spending five days at the hospital, and visitors continued to stream in at my house. I had company all day long. Two precious ladies from our church were with me at my house for many weeks. They did the cooking, laundry, just name it, as long as it was in the category of house work. I never paid them because I couldn't. That is what I call friendship. *Thank you Brenda and Unifa. When I become rich, we will take a trip; a tour through the Caribbean Islands. Three of us alone.*

Hyperactive again

After taking the drug, Amitriptylline for (6) six weeks, I became hyperactive. I felt that I was regaining my physical strength and something was happening to me that up to this day I cannot comprehend. I seemed to have been in a trance, but I was wide awake and experienced something like being in hell. I felt tormented. Things were colliding, and I had no control of my thoughts. I saw that everyone was against me including the members of my family. I was terribly afraid. Every sin that I could remember committing flashed before me. I felt alone.

The hardest blow was when my children ignored my instructions, and my husband turned his back on me. I was awestruck; I did not know what to do. People were just standing around me and jeering at me, and it appeared that I was the centre of attraction. I saw my husband driving me to a mental institution, and all how I screamed to him that I did not want to go there, he did not listen to me and brought me there. I became a patient, and the inmates were taking advantage of me. I remember being so afraid that I did not know what to do. I had flashes of my Junior Choir in heaven, immaculately dressed, and playing all types of musical instruments. I saw even the youngest child in the choir playing a musical instrument at age two. He played it in an impeccable manner. The youngest child was the leader of the choir, and as he led them in a march, all in heaven stood still. There was perfect order. Everyone was happy, and there was music all over heaven. I stayed in hell, and watched from afar off. I felt that I was going crazy.

After those scenes, I began to behave in a violent manner, and did things that I would not do under normal circumstances. I was taken to Barbados, and while on the airport awaiting the aircraft, I was so afraid, that I buried my head between my legs. I thought the things that I was viewing were real. I kept asking my husband if he cared about me, and whether he would stay close to me and wouldn't leave. He was there all the time, reassuring me that he belonged at my side, and that was where he was going to stay. I drew as close to him as I possibly could. There were other concerned folks there supporting us. I recall seeing Pastor Griffith by my husband's side. People from other churches were there. My husband needed that, and I thank God for those people.

While I was on the plane, another thing happened that still have me perplexed. I was saying things inaudibly, and everything that I said came to pass. For example, I saw the plane going faster than it should, and I would ask that it would slow down, and it did. I ordered parachutes to descend with people in them, since to me everyone was in danger, and that happened. Meanwhile, I saw everyone on the plane looking at me, and making fun of me. That was not real, but that was what I saw. Everyone in the plane was heading for heaven, and I was the only one in hell. My God, I was miserable. I was so tormented that the thoughts of that day make me shiver to this day.

I was taken to Barbados, and as I arrived there, I held on to my husband for fear that what I saw came to reality. When the immigration officer asked if I was with him, I quickly answered that I was, just in case that something that I had dreaded happened. We left the airport, and as usual, Trevor was there to rescue us. I dozed off from the airport to the house. I remember there was music in the car. It sounded so enlightening, and I asked to lower the volume. My head was in my husband's lap. When I arrived at the house after fifteen minutes drive, I remember telling my husband that I was feeling weak and sleepy. I got out of the car, and before my husband could even hold my hand, I fell, scraping my knees. My husband and friend, Trevor, carried me into the house. I was taken into the spare room which I regarded as my own room. I fell asleep, and slept for many hours.

The Happiest Moment of My Life

When I awoke the next morning, everything had changed. I turned and saw my husband next to me, and it seemed that I had regained my senses. The first thing I uttered to him was, "Myrl, please tell me that all that I went through yesterday was a dream." He said, "Yes sweetheart, it was a dream." I blinked my eyes to confirm that I was not sleeping, and the joy and relief that I experienced was indescribable. I quickly assumed my usual and favorite position; that is, lying on my husband's chest. The love that I felt for him was so real. The contentment I experienced was that, I had not lost my family, or my mind. I had no words to describe this feeling.

We had to hurry to see the psychiatrist at his office for seven o'clock. The doctor was very nice. I was ticking again, and all questions were answered intelligently. He gave me a choice as to whether I wanted to be admitted to the Queen Elizabeth Hospital or be an out patient. I requested to see the hospital room. I was taken there and from a glance, I did not like it. Both males and females were in one big ward, and that was not to my liking. I would have preferred a room to myself. I needed privacy. I told the nurses that I did not like it. They encouraged me to stay. They seemed to be friendly, and the atmosphere was warm.

They informed me that the patients there had experienced similar problems, and that counseling was available. They pointed out that if I came in for the treatment everyday as an out patient I would not be exposed to counseling. They reassured me that I would not regret being there. I changed my mind and opted to stay. I also thought that my husband deserved a break from me in order to get his thoughts together. He was totally stressed out, and it is only The Almighty that was keeping him and allowing him to maintain his sanity in the midst of all this.

I had a ball at the hospital. The patients there were open and friendly. We spoke openly of our predicament, since we all were 'in the same boat'. Many of them attempted suicide. One almost drank gramaxzone (that was her fourth attempt), and she said she did not know why someone always found her. One tried to slit his wrist, one jumped down a deep pit. Another got depressed because her child came on holiday in Barbados, and he got drowned in the hotel's swimming pool, etc. I was treated for eight days and was allowed to return home for Christmas. My energy level had risen by then, and I had started to become the Morella that people knew. My family had me back, and we had a splendid Christmas. I went back to Barbados after spending four days at home, and returned to the hospital.

When I was re-admitted, I began to write again. I wrote numerous letters, and began writing my first book, Destined to Live. I also began reading again, and that felt good. It also reassured me that I was returning to my old self. I met a few doctors in Barbados, and all of them were helpful. I believe that God ordained it. The doctors told me that I was intelligent. For this, I was grateful. That was not news anyway (I'm flattering myself). I was discharged after a few days and returned home, feeling really good and energized. I was a bit hyperactive, and up to now as I write seven months later, 'I have a short fuse'. I get upset easily, and of course, 'tell people off' whenever I feel that they need it, even though I have to apologize later. I am praying that I get over this phase because I prefer to be assertive than aggressive. It makes everyone happier, especially my dear husband. I returned to work on March 3rd 1999. I feel much better, and enjoy work to the fullest. My family is happy, my friends have me back, and I give God the praise. He is so awesome, and I love Him.

Suddenly I love Work

I returned to work just in time for the re-launching of the New National Insurance Scheme. We now have a new energetic director, and things are really booming. When I was sick, my workmates would say things like "Reecie, you're there, but you're not there, please rejoin us." "Moys, Moys, I give you two weeks to begin to bring coconut cake for us." "Moy, you don't know any jokes again?" I am back, and they have their hands full. We are working as usual as a team, to give the best service to our clients to whom we are obligated.

I wake up on a morning, and I can hardly wait to get to work. I like work all of a sudden. On weekends, I am eager to be at the office. I thank God that many things are happening these days. Training sessions for all staff, monthly staff meetings, and restructuring among other things. I like our new director. She is a precious gem, and most of us believe that she is a gift from God. The former director is my friend too. We had our fights, but I respect him. He must have been doing good things, for the government of 'Fair Helen' to have kept him at the helm of this valuable institution for twenty-seven (27) years. I saw a very good side of Mr. Compton when I was ill and suffering from the first bout of depression. He actually fathered me. We were so close, that if I was not a 'straight woman' morally, one would have thought otherwise. I will never forget how good he was to me as long as I live.

Things are back to Normal

I have regained the weight that I lost, and I have put on some extra pounds. I am not happy about this because I do not like anything shaking when I am walking. I go to the gym because I am determined to lose the extra pounds. I thank God that I did not lose my hair during chemotherapy. My doctor explained that he had used a drug which would prevent the hair from dropping off. I hate wigs. I would have worn them anyway. Better wear wigs than to be six feet deep.

I am also thankful to God that I did not have a mastectomy. I don't know how I would cope with one breast. Better that than to be dead. I would have coped also. I now look good. So says the mirror, my husband, my friends and a few admirers. A cute Christian lawyer at my workplace also told me so recently. She remarked, "Morella, when I look at you, I see a miracle." I believe her. Whoever had seen me in my depressed state during my treatment for the cancer, will see a miracle in the way I now look.

I do not remember the marks unless I look for them, people just do not ask me about them. They either do not see them, or they are too embarrassed to ask. My Omniscient Father has taken the shame, and I am not ashamed of them. I speak about the incident at ease, and people get goose bumps when I speak, but I don't. That must be God's strength flowing through me. I get chills every time I remember any of the acts. I cringe all the time because I can't believe that I inflicted the wounds which these marks reveal. However, since both my doctor and my husband have reassured me that I did not do them, I believe that and feel good. I really could not have done that. I can't even stand the thought.

I am grateful to God that I did not die. I do not want or desire to go through that again because it was too traumatic. Nevertheless, if it be the Lord's will that I go through that again, I say, let His will be done. I prefer to go through ten bouts of depression and be diagnosed with cancer six times or more than go to hell. As long as God is going with me, I am willing to face it. If I am given a choice, the answer will be an emphatic no, but all in all, I just want to please Him.

My husband is back on track, and I thank God so much for him. I do not know what I would do if I had an insensitive man for a husband. I do not know what I would have done either, if he had turned his back on me when I needed him most. I thank God that he was always there even when he was not welcomed. I leaned heavily on him, and I can tell you this man is strong. He bore the strain without complaining. What a man!! He is second to none. I always knew that I married a gentleman. If I had found out otherwise, I would not have stayed in the relationship. Merlin has proven it so many times that 'he is for real'.

When I was ill, my husband would hurry to do the errands, and hurry back home just to be with me. This happened for approximately fifteen months. He provided all monies for medicines, and monitored me to ensure that I drank them. He juiced my vegetables and bought me nutritious foods and vitamins. In fact, everything someone told him that was good for me, he purchased it. I sometimes said to myself, "Why is this man buying me all this, can't he see that I am dying?" I thought that it was all going to waste. I was wrong. I believe with all my heart that God was guiding him.

When it came to being intimate with my husband, it was like a mountain to climb. I procrastinated all the time. That man is so patient. When my husband made love to me, I was so ashamed of my body that I endured it but did not enjoy it. I wondered how he could desire 'a bag of bones'. That's how I saw myself. Although my gynecologist once told me, whilst seeking his advice to gain ten pounds, "Don't you know that the closer the flesh is to the bone the sweeter the meat?" However, I now realize that Merlin saw beyond my body. He saw me, the wife that he had grown to love for over twenty years. He saw my abilities, my strengths, and all what made me Morella. My husband saw the entire me. People often look at me and harp, "Morella, you really have a good husband." I agree with them, but I always tell them that he has a very good wife, too.

My children's grades have improved, and I am happy. They are extremely happy that I am well again. They are vibrant, always asking to go somewhere, and are enjoying life to the fullest. I am so happy that they have picked up from where they left off, and that everybody is ticking again. The vibrancy and energy is back. The laughter is back, thank God. It appeared that everyone was waiting for me. As my cousin once said to me, "A woman is the steering wheel in the family." The man is in charge of the car, and the direction that it should take. Even the church seemed sick when I was ill. I guess, since I was not well, my husband, being one of the senior pastors could not function as well as he should. We have resurrected, and our God is working wonders among us. To Him be all the glory and praise. I can now look back and say like the songwriter, "Look what the Lord has done. He healed my body, He touched my mind, He saved me just in time. I'm gonna praise His name, every day is just the same, come on and help me sing, LOOK WHAT THE LORD HAS DONE."

Cutlass (Machete) Attack

In February, 1999, I attended a religious service at the City Hall. Charlene had to attend a rehearsal at another church to practice some songs for the visit of Ron Kenoly. She had informed us that she felt so tired that she would borrow the vehicle, and if she gets a ride to our home, park it near the city hall, and go home. When it was 9:00 p.m., I remembered her, and Jason and I went to check whether she had brought the vehicle back, or whether she had fallen asleep in it since she was so tired. When we peeped into the vehicle, she was not there, so we assumed that she was at home as promised. Jason and I were returning to the hall when we noticed a man hurriedly walking in the dark and coming towards us with a real sharp cutlass (the edge was like silver, and it was shining in the dark). I stepped aside to give the man sufficient room to pass, and he, too stepped aside, and aligned himself with me. I said to myself, "Well I'm dead tonight." When he got close (about one foot away), he said in a hurried manner, "give me all the money you have now!!" By then, Jason had run, and was shouting at the top of his voice, "Mummy run, don't let the man chop you, run mummy, run." I said to the man, "I don't have money on me, but I can get some for you." I was so afraid, I hardly knew what to say.

Jason was still shouting the same thing. The man then raised the cutlass and said, "I tell you to give me all the money you have." I felt the man's breath on my face and his cutlass was a few centimeters from my neck. Thoughts were racing in my mind—grab the cutlass and do something with him; run; put a Tae-Bo (form of exercise) on him; scream. When the thought scream came, I responded immediately. I realized that I should use that weapon—my voice. Something said to me, "Morella this could be your last scream, bellow it out."

I began screaming at the top of my lungs. The man immediately lowered his cutlass and grabbed my chain. He said as he grabbed it, "Give me that 'F' chain man, give me that 'F' chain." He ran. Jason was still screaming. The man stopped and said to Jason, "Shut up your mouth and go and sleep boy." Jason run towards me trembling from head to toe. "Lets run mummy." I told him that he was safe and that there was no need to run. Jason insisted, "Let's run, mummy let's run." I held his hand and run with him until we reached the front of the hall. "Well, well, well," I said, "devil you just won't give up on me." He was really wasting his time. I did not report the incident to the police, for I felt that it was a waste of time, and too minor to report. Boy, I am destined to live. I seem to be like a cat. I have many lives.

CHAPTER SEVEN

TO ALL CANCER PATIENTS

Finally, my prayer to those who may be suffering from that deadly disease, cancer, is that you will realize that there is a God somewhere above the heavens who cares. There is a cure for cancer—God. Nothing is impossible with Him. Do not give up. Your attitude towards this disease is important. My attitude was rotten. Yours doesn't have to be the same. You can be positive and look up, knowing that there is a God who can heal all manner of diseases.

There are many folks walking down the streets today who were diagnosed with this dreadful disease many years ago. Some have survived for five years, some ten, some twenty, some fifty and over. Some die after living a long life, and they die from another cause, not necessarily from cancer. You can live. It is said that early detection is the best protection. If it is detected late, there still could be some hope.

My prayer is that medical science will find a cure for this deadly disease, and that we will all live our lives free from the fear of cancer. I would like to admonish everyone to get acquainted with their bodies. In the event that there is an abnormality, you will be the first one to detect it. It is said that most breast lumps are detected by women themselves. Breast self examination (BSE) is very important, and has helped a great percentage of women detect lumps even before mammograms. Many of us allow our doctors or spouses to know our bodies better than us. We need to take charge of our health.

It is said that women are more prone to caring and sharing. We take care of our spouses, our children, parents, relatives, friends and neighbors, except ourselves. If we continue to do so, we may not be around for a long time to continue. We need to take time out for ourselves. Someone said "pull aside and park". Every now and then, let us make time for ourselves. Someone else said, "Have an International Day of _____" Put your name on this blank space.

Lastly, I once visited the hospital on the invitation of my friend, Sandra, who asked me to accompany her in visiting a young woman at the hospital, who seemed to be dying from cancer. We went to pray with her. When I arrived, I saw someone looking like sixty or more in the ward. She was completely bald, and was extremely thin. I said to my friend, "I thought you said a young woman." "Yes," Sandra replied, "She is only twenty something years." I was shocked. The young, 'old lady' was vomiting blood, and had just had chemotherapy. My heart hurt when I saw her. We prayed with her and when we left the hospital, to be honest, I thought that she would have died sooner than later. I saw her again after about two years. She had gained weight, had long bouncing hair, and was living happily. I was really happy for her.

The second example is the story of a Grenadian woman who was so sick with cancer that she began having an offensive odor. When people went to visit her, they had to hold their noses. That lady revived, and is living a happy life. God is truly the author of life. The doctors do not have the last word. Someone said, "It is not over until God says that it is over." Your attitude towards this illness is very, very important. I came across an article on attitude on August 14th, 1997 and I would like to share it with you.

@@@@@@@@@@@@@@@@@@@@@@@@@@@@@@@@@@@@@@

ATTITUDE

The longer I live, the more I realize the impact of attitude on my life. Attitude to me is more important than facts. It is more important than the past, than education, than money, than circumstances, than failures, than successes, than what other people think or say or do. It is more important than appearance, giftedness or skill. It will make or break a company—a church—home. The remarkable thing is we have a choice everyday regarding the attitude we will embrace for that day. We cannot change our past—we cannot change the fact that people will act in a certain way—we cannot change the inevitable. The only thing we can do is play on the one string we have, and that is our attitude—I am convinced that life is 10% what happens to me—and—90% how I react to it. And so it is with you.

We are in charge of our attitudes.

By Charles Swindoll

@@@@@@@@@@@@@@@@@@@@@@@@@@@@@@@@@@@@@@

CHAPTER EIGHT

MY HUSBAND'S CHAPTER

The following extracts are from Merlin's diary. He has a habit of writing letters to God. The writings below are direct extracts. The date that my husband recorded in his diary was correct. He dreamt of the month and day but not the year. Merlin assumed the year was 1997, since he was experiencing so much pain with all that was going on in our lives.

We realized that the year was 1998, which proves that God is a God of timing. On that date, December 15th 1998, it appeared that "all hell broke loose" against us. That was the day on which I completely lost my mind for twenty four hours. On that same day we traveled to Barbados. When we connect information from the dream to the events, it was the beginning of our breakthrough and deliverance. Since that date, I have been getting better, and better.

Charlene Reece

Charlene Reece smiling

Darwin, Charlene and Jason

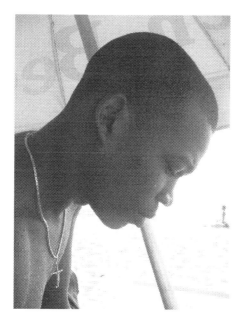

Darwin on the beach

Merlin and members of his family

Merlin DaCosta Reece

Mrs. Reece

My mother Sarah

Myself and Merlin's family

Teddy-son, Charlene and Darwin

Extracts from Merlin's Diary

December 17, 1997

On December 15th, 1997, I looked in anticipation for God to do something miraculous in my life. He had given me this date in a dream since August. In that dream I was given a bunch of keys by an older man, who was going on a far journey—He informed me that he would arrive at his destination on this date of December 15th. I left for work that morning, leaving Morella home—not looking so bright, but with hope in her heart. During the course of that day, I went to Cable and Wireless to pay a bill for the church. On my way out, I met Pastor David Tommy. We spoke for a good while. I mentioned that Morella had had surgery and was at home. When he heard the nature of the surgery, he gave me some examples of others who had overcome that same situation and were very much alive and actively fighting this battle of spiritual warfare. He said we must quote the word on a daily basis, look away from the situation, and look to God. Repeat that word until it gets into our spirit. That word is spirit, and it is life. Do not fail to confess it in every situation.

At the end of the day when I went to bed, very close to midnight, I was still expecting a miracle. However, after midnight had gone I thought and reflected on the day to see if I had missed something that God had done. It was then that it occurred to me that keys mean authority and that the authority given to me, was the authority of the word (The power of the word). I must use the keys to prosperity whether spiritual, physical, financial or otherwise. Agreeing with God's word, affirming and confirming it with faith brings the blessings of God upon our lives. God is faithful. He wants the best for us every day of our lives. I look forward to the day when God will grant us the answer to our prayer for a financial gift. We have been praying now for over two months for a financial breakthrough. I thank the Lord for his faithfulness.

11:45 am December 17th

THE THINGS THAT ARE VISIBLE ARE TEMPORAL—But the things that are not seen are eternal.

Sitting here at my desk trying to forge ahead with my work, many thoughts pass through my mind. I find myself calling friends on the phone to chat for a while. I try to occupy my mind with positive thoughts. Clearly before me, is a picture of Morella as I left her this morning—Somewhere behind this picture is another picture of Morella. The real Morella, the one I love and admire deeply. I ignore most of these thoughts and reflect on the word of God implanted in my heart: The promises that God has given to his children to appropriate. I see a pleasant and prosperous future as I apply this word to our present situation. The things I see with my physical eyes are only temporal, but what I am seeing in the spirit is everlasting.

God is faithful and will never leave us nor forsake us. He will see us through. Morella is healed by the stripes of Jesus. She is well by God's grace. No weapon formed against us shall prosper. Weeping may endure for a night, but joy comes in the morning. Our morning is here. The word says "many are the afflictions of the righteous but the Lord delivers them out of them all". We have been delivered,—set free. God is doing a new thing in our lives. I believe Him and trust Him to bring it to completion.

God be praised for His goodness and mercies and for placing certain people in our path to serve us at such a time as this. Thank you Lord.

Most people on reading thus far must be wondering how did the immediate family, cope with the unpleasant events of the past seven years. As husband, father and pastor, I hasten to say that it was not easy. I felt the effects upon my family and paid a price. There were many nights of, "Why Lord? When will this end? What about your promises?" I was running a home, doing my secular work, and being pastor of a church. During the church services, there was peace and ecstasy while worshipping, but after the services the situation seemed the same.

During Morella's first bout of depression, there were times of anxiety, not knowing what will happen next. I can vividly remember one morning at about 8:30a.m., I sat in the living room, my heart was palpitating, and my breathing was erratic. It appeared that I was losing the fight. My strength was gone. I needed help.

After taking a deep breath, I paused and called upon the Lord. My words were, "Father, I cannot handle this, it is too much for me, help me." Instantly, I experienced the peace of God as it engulfed my entire body. Peace that is beyond verbal explanation. The situation was still present, but I felt that God was in charge. I saw the whole situation in a different light, and felt that I could face anything with Him in control. That was the beginning of a very intimate friendship with Him. It was easy to spend long hours at nights conversing with the Lord. I would pour out my soul to Him and tell Him anything. He certainly cares about every detail of our lives.

All is Well

God reminded me of a time when a Canadian minister visited our church. After preaching, he called out my wife and I and said, "I do not know what the two of you are going through at this time, but God is saying to you, 'ALL IS WELL'." I believe that God was preparing us for the testing times that were ahead, but we did not understand. When He reminded me of this particular occasion, it was then that I saw His deep concern for us and all of his children. These words have been an added source of strength and comfort. Although, I must admit that there were times when my faith wavered. Since then, that phrase has formed part of our vocabulary. Instead of asking people "how are you?" we ask, "all is well?"

In times of crises, God always provides a shoulder for us to lean on; some people who stick with you through 'thick and thin'. He provided for my family some loyal friends whose names I will not mention. They gave us the support that was much needed. My prayer habits continued for years, and I still look forward to meet with my Father in the early hours of the morning. In the early months of 1997, I began writing letters to God. For me, this is a good way of communicating because later on, I would read these letters and see how my petitions were answered. God also gave guidance as He spoke to me in dreams, and would show me how to deal with situations which I would encounter. Many times I would not remember the dream until the situation presented itself. Very often, He would give me dates and figures.

Morella's second bout of depression was brought on by the news of being diagnosed with breast cancer. That was a real test of my faith. It appeared that everything came to a stand still for my family, while the whole world moved ahead rapidly. Yes, we were alive, but were just going through the motions of everyday living. It was difficult. I watched as my children's grades dropped. The expressions of joy and laughter which was the norm around our house became occasional. The excitement and sparkle in their eyes dwindled. For Morella, it was a series of tests, operations, regular visits to the medical doctor, the psychiatrist and the psychotherapist. For me there were headaches, caused by the situation coupled with financial struggles.

Given the complexity of what my family was facing, I believe that I was in a better spiritual condition to handle whatever was coming my way. This whole series of events was as I see it a test of my faith in an Omnipotent, Omniscient and Omnipresent God. Faith kept me going. I am reminded of the words of a song which says that faith cannot be unanswered. The author is unknown.

Unanswered Yet?

The prayer your lips have pleaded?
In agony of heart, these many years?
Doth faith begin to fail? Is hope departing?
And think you all in vain those many tears?
Say not, the Father has not heard your prayer.
You shall have your desire, sometime, somewhere.

Unanswered yet?

Though when you first presented,
This one petition at the Father's throne,
It seemed you could not wait the time of asking.
So urgent was your heart to make known.
Though tears have passed since then, do not despair.
The Lord will answer you, sometime, somewhere.

Unanswered yet?

Nay do not say, "ungranted;"
Perhaps your part is not yet wholly done;
The work began when first your prayer was uttered,
And God will finish what He has begun;
If you will keep the incense burning there,
His glory you shall see sometime, somewhere.

Unanswered yet?

Faith cannot be answered;
His feet are firmly planted on the rock.
Amidst the wildest storms she stands undaunted,
Nor quails before the loudest thunder shock.
She knows Omnipotence has heard her prayer,
And cries, "It shall be done" sometime, somewhere.

Many friends and relatives sympathized and supported us in some ways. Others did not know what to say. Some would say, "Man how could you survive? You have more than your fair share." I know that I could not have done anything in myself to alter the situation. My family could never have survived this onslaught without the help of God. Our strength, our hope and our faith is in Almighty God who loves us dearly.

CHAPTER NINE

MY SON'S CHAPTER

This chapter represents some of the experiences of my son, Darwin. Charlene's experiences are still locked up in her heart, and she will not express her feelings as my son would.

Darwin

As far as I can remember, my childhood days were normal and happy. I can recall the many times my whole family played various games, 'ride the donkey', cricket, swings and basket ball. My father built us basketball poles and swings which are still at our old house up to this day.

Our presence in the family was very important. Whenever decisions had to be made, we, the children were always included. We prayed together, we also had family meetings once a month pertaining to the family. These meetings still take place today whenever the need arises. My mother also made it her duty for our family to have meals together. These experiences helped to keep us close to each other.

My mother's illness had a very great impact on my life. During the first bout of her depression, I was only nine years old, but I can recall some of my sad experiences. I remember in particular, when my birthday came, I was expecting to have a cake to take to my classmates, since this was the norm. That day, I woke up and realized that there was no sign of any cake on the table. I felt that something was really wrong. My mother was really sick and that made me very sad. My dad tried to comfort me by buying a cake for me to take to school, but it was not the same.

During the second bout of my mother's depression, I was in form three, a very critical time for me at school. I felt that my future was at stake because nothing was normal in my family anymore. We were just going through the motions of living everyday.

One day 'all hell broke loose'. My mother seemed to have 'lost it'. I woke up very early that day, and was sitting on my bed thinking—just thinking. There was a lot of commotion outside my bedroom. I remember at one point, Sister Collymore came into my room, and when she saw me in a pensive mood, she asked me, "Dow, what do you think or have to say about all this?" I shrugged my shoulders, not knowing what to say. She posed the question again and I responded with two words: "WHAT NEXT?"

Later on, she told my mother that those words pierced through her like a dagger. I remember her words after I had responded to her question. "Darwin, you know what next,—God is going to heal your mother, and when she returns from Barbados, she will be normal and healthy again. That is what will happen next." She asked me whether I believed what she told me and to this I answered, yes.

I lived to see it happen. After my mother had spent a few days in Barbados, my dad called to tell us that she was going to be OK and that 'All is well'. I can attest to the fact that the Almighty God is a great healer.

I got my mother back, and I am very happy that she is alive today because she is an important role model in my family and my life.

A Note From My late Brother,

Pastor and Bishop

To everyone who reads this book, I sincerely trust that you shall understand the purpose for which it was written. The powerful experience of the author is shared from her heart without any dilution. As her pastor, I personally witnessed, and in some instances shared some of the very painful experiences, as the church prayed and fasted on her behalf.

May the contents of this book bring comfort and hope to all who might be experiencing times of oppression and depression from the enemy. Some of you might be contemplating suicide right now.

BUT STOP!!!

LIKE THE AUTHOR SAID, THERE IS A WAY OUT

THERE IS HOPE. JESUS IS THE ANSWER TO

ALL YOUR QUESTIONS, AND A SOLUTION

TO ALL YOUR PROBLEMS.

Bishop A.C.Collymore

My brother went home to meet his Maker, His Father, His God, on June 25th, 2003.

A Note From My 'Good Friend'
Josephine Romain

I have known Morella since November, 1989 as an energetic, generous, self-sacrificing and caring person. Over the years, those qualities remained constant in her. So when she was told by the doctor that the lump was malignant, she could not accept it. She had too many dreams to fulfill, too many persons to serve, but moreso she was not ready to go. Her body and mind could not withstand the harsh realities, so they simply revolted.

I can remember the night Morella came to my home. She told me she wanted us to go out because she had something to say to me. We bought some food at our favorite restaurant and proceeded to the lookout point on Morne Fortune. The food tasted like dog food. We could not eat it. Little did I know that the revelation which was to be made would leave an uglier taste in my mouth.

Morella told me that the doctor at the Cancer Society was suspicious about a lump that she had in her breast. She, therefore, asked her to seek confirmation from another doctor. We talked about persons, including friends whom she knew had succumbed to the disease. She gave lurid details about their deterioration and their subsequent death. I have never actually witnessed a person dying from cancer so for the moment, I imagined what it would be like to see my friend confined to a bed. The thought and sight was too much to accept. We talked about her fears, the sickness and death. She said that she was afraid of being sick, of being immobilized, of not being able to realize her dreams, and of not being able to see her children grow up. But she was not necessarily afraid to die. Not much more was said because we had no interest in any other matter. We then departed to our homes.

The other tests confirmed that Morella's lump was malignant, much to our surprise. What happened in the days to come as Morella recounted in this book was never anticipated neither by herself, her husband or any of the persons closely associated with her.

Thank God He delivered her from all this trauma, and has given her a testimony so that hope can be brought to all sufferers, be it cancer or any life threatening situation.

May I leave some pointers with you dear reader:

(1) God has a purpose for this situation even if He takes you home. His concept of death and loss is quite different to ours.
(2) Victims are not selected by God from the stand point of 'goodness' 'badness' or favoritism.
(3) God calls us to be always in a state of readiness.

RESPONSE FROM READERS OF THE PREVIOUS EDITION OF *DESTINED TO LIVE*

Destined to Live was launched on Saturday, 4th December, 1999, and since then, I have been receiving many letters from readers on their experiences after reading the book. The following represents extracts from some of these letters:

With each page that I turned, the events of your life held me in stoned silence and pure admiration . . . I had never known that depression could be so destructive . . . As I read on further, I realized that without your family, you would not have been able to beat this. Your home life served as a pillar of hope somehow. I am filled with admiration for your husband who was your pillar of strength during those critical times, and who never left your side . . . I think your book is a source of inspiration for anyone who is going through any type of hardship in their lives.

Feona Jean

A story of courage and faith in God. Deeply moving . . . Mrs Reece is truly an inspiration to us all.

Dr. Tanya Destang Beaubrun

I enjoyed reading your book. It is a story filled with courage, determination and trust in Divine Providence. I wish you and your family much happiness and all my love.

Delia Frederick

Congratulations for producing such a provoking masterpiece— 'Destined to Live'. What an impact your book has created on my life, an everlasting image upon reflection.

Cleo Johnny

I am deeply inspired by your experience and testimony . . . Morella, may your book be an inspiration to all who read it, and above all, a powerful tool of salvation and deliverance . . .

Cecilia Allain

This book was well documented with much humor which contrasted with the serious portion of it. I personally think that it will be a great inspiration to anyone who was, and still is afflicted with those two horrible diseases. Faith in a Risen God is the key. Waiting on Him is paramount . . . . that was truly a test of your faith . . . .

Sylvester Reece

I felt tremendous passion for you as I read your book, and I was overwhelmed by your varied experiences. Clearly, though, you are a great woman.

Hon. Mathew Vernon Roberts

You are truly an example to tell others that past experiences do not cancel future assignments. CRISIS definitely gives birth to VISION and prepares us for promotion.

Patricia Beaton

Complete, everyone needs to read it. This chronicle challenges us to be courageous, confident, compassionate and Christlike. It is a life picture of the liberating principle that "in all things, we are more than conquerors through Jesus Christ who loved us".

Pastor Sherwin Griffith

A moving personal story. Written with great humor, love and simplicity. The book offers a rich description of the problems faced by a person who has been afflicted with depression and cancer.

The courage and faith depicted should be a shining light for others in a world where things are taken for granted.

It is a triumph

Emma Hippolyte

'Destined to Live' reads as a lively account in the life of a fighter and survivor. Morella Reece's courage in the face of many odds, her triumph over cancer and depression; her tenacious and irrepressible spirit; and her continued celebration of life remind us that the fact of our survival of life's tribulation is itself an act of faith.

Dr Antonia Mac Donald-Smythe

A very emotional book. Not only in terms of its subject, but also for the message of hope, love, endurance, trust, forgiveness and perseverance. It gives hope to the sick and lonely, the dispirited, the afflicted, family, friends and support groups. The Author is a living example that in every desert of trial, God has an oasis of comfort.

Mary Relle Hippolyte

NOTES

Francisca Morella Reece is the daughter of Sarah Ishmael and the late Pearson Collymore. She is the wife of Pastor Merlin Da Costa Reece; a former School Administrator, and the biological mother of two offspring; Charlene Morella Reece, and Darwin Da Costa Reece.

Morella is a Sunday School teacher whose ministry is with children. She is the director of the Junior Choir of her local church, and is also a preacher. She works alongside her husband in the Ministry, and is a member of the local Church Board, and Church Council.

Morella is a Conference Speaker. Her testimony has taken her places including Barbados, Canada, the USA; and she continually shares her experiences in many local churches and gatherings, upon request.

At present Mrs Reece is an employee of the National Insurance Corporation, (Social Security Administration) in St Lucia. She works there as an Investigating Officer and is attached to the Customer Service Department. She is also an Executive Member of the Toastmasters Club at her work place.

Morella's hope and dream is that she will be self employed and the founder of a National Adventure Park for children and youth, where they can go and have a day or night of clean fun. She also dreams of building a home for the under-privileged children of her country. Morella's prayer is that God will use her writing skills to help her achieve those goals, before *she makes her exit from planet earth.*

Postal address: **P.O. Box 1038**
Castries
St Lucia
West Indies

Telephone: **758 450 4467**

Email: *mollymer@hotmail.com*

Web site: